REVISE EDEXCEL GCSE (9–1)

English Language

REVISION GUIDE

Series Consultant: Harry Smith

Author: Esther Menon

A note from the publisher

In order to ensure that this resource offers high-quality support for the associated Pearson qualification, it has been through a review process by the awarding body. This process confirms that this resource fully covers the teaching and learning content of the specification or part of a specification at which it is aimed. It also confirms that it demonstrates an appropriate balance between the development of subject skills, knowledge and understanding, in addition to preparation for assessment.

Endorsement does not cover any guidance on assessment activities or processes (e.g. practice questions or advice on how to answer assessment questions), included in the resource nor does it prescribe any particular approach to the teaching or delivery of a related course.

While the publishers have made every attempt to ensure that advice on the qualification and its assessment is accurate, the official specification and associated assessment guidance materials are the only authoritative source of information and should always be referred to for definitive guidance.

Pearson examiners have not contributed to any sections in this resource relevant to examination papers for which they have responsibility.

Examiners will not use endorsed resources as a source of material for any assessment set by Pearson.

Endorsement of a resource does not mean that the resource is required to achieve this Pearson qualification, nor does it mean that it is the only suitable material available to support the qualification, and any resource lists produced by the awarding body shall include this and other appropriate resources.

For the full range of Pearson revision titles across KS2, KS3, GCSE, Functional Skills, AS/A Level and BTEC visit:
www.pearsonschools.co.uk/revise

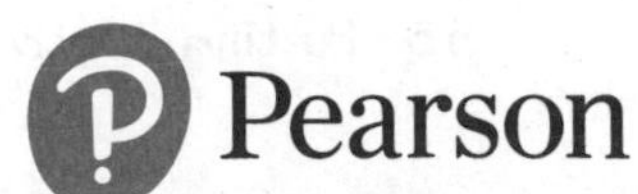

Contents

1-to-1 page match with the English Language Revision Workbook ISBN 9781447987949

Edexcel publishes Sample Assessment Material and the Specification on its website. This is the official content and this book should be used in conjunction with it. The questions in *Now try this* have been written to help you practise every topic in the book. Remember: the real exam questions may not look like this.

Planning your exam time

Planning your time in the exam is extremely important. Running out of time is one of the most common ways that students lose marks in their exam. You should plan your time to get the most out of every minute.

The exam papers

The English Language GCSE consists of two exam papers. Paper 1 (Fiction and Imaginative Writing) is worth 40% of your GCSE, and **Paper 2** (Non-fiction and Transactional Writing) is worth 60%.

See pages 47–95 for more about writing

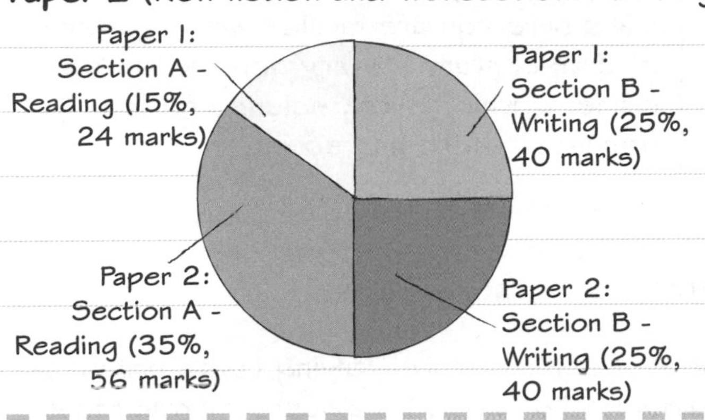

Paper 1 – 1 hour and 45 minutes
You could spend:
- 10 minutes reading the texts and questions
- 50 minutes answering Section A
- 10 minutes planning Section B
- 35 minutes writing.

Paper 2 – 2 hours
You could spend:
- 15 minutes reading the texts and questions
- 60 minutes answering Section A
- 10 minutes planning Section B
- 35 minutes writing.

Reading time

Start each exam paper by reading the texts and questions:

- Paper 1 – read for the **first 10 minutes**
- Paper 2 – read for the **first 15 minutes**.

For example:

1. **Read the questions** to find out what you need to look for when you read the texts.
2. **Skim read** the texts to get a sense of the main ideas and themes.
3. **Read the texts again, carefully,** this time annotating them when you find information you will need in your answers.

How long to spend on a question?

Work out how long you need to spend on Question 7 (a) **(6 marks)** in **Paper 2: Section A – Reading**.

Section A should take 60 minutes after the reading time, so that gives me about 1 minute per mark. If Question 7 (a) is worth 6 marks, I could spend about 6 minutes answering and checking it. Alternatively, if I spend 1 minute less on each question, I could save about 7 minutes and use the time at the end to double check all my answers!

Getting it right

This reading time is important, and so is any time you have left after answering the questions. When you've finished writing, use any spare time to check and proofread your work.

Now try this

Work out how long to spend on Question 4 in **Paper 1: Section A – Reading**, which is worth 15 marks.

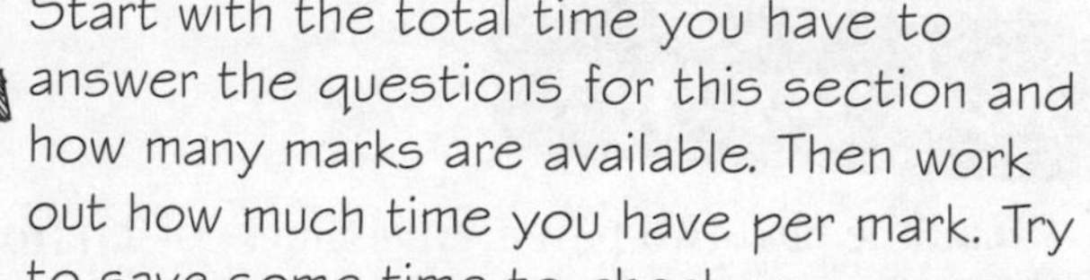

Start with the total time you have to answer the questions for this section and how many marks are available. Then work out how much time you have per mark. Try to save some time to check your answers.

Had a look Nearly there Nailed it!

Reading texts explained

You will sit two papers for your exam: **Paper 1** and **Paper 2**. Each one has a **reading** section (Section A) and a **writing** section (Section B). You will meet different types of text in each.

Paper 1: Section A – Reading

This will have an extract from **one** work of **prose fiction** written in the **19th century**. The extract will be approximately 650 words long. It could be from any literary genre.

Improving your fiction reading

Prepare by reading widely and independently outside lesson time, and make sure you are familiar with a variety of 19th-century literary genres, such as crime, gothic horror, science fiction, romance, satire and so on.

Extract from The Half-Brothers. *Full text on page 99. Lines 18–22.*

To save myself from shedding tears, I shouted—terrible, wild shouts for bare life they were. I turned sick as I paused to listen; no answering sound came but the unfeeling echoes. Only the noiseless, pitiless snow kept falling thicker, thicker—faster, faster! I was growing numb and sleepy. I tried to move about, but I dared not go far, for fear of the precipices which, I knew, abounded in certain places on the Fells.

As you read, start to think about **how** and **why** the writer has created particular **characters** and **atmospheres.**

Narrator is desperately trying to be brave, but 'terrible, wild shouts' suggests extreme fear.

Suggests total silence, 'unfeeling' and 'pitiless' emphasises harsh setting and suggests no hope of rescue.

'Precipices' suggests a sheer drop, the narrator cannot even move to save herself.

Paper 2: Section A – Reading

You will be given **two non-fiction** texts of about 1000 words in total. One will be from the **20th century**, the other from the **21st century**.

Improving your non-fiction reading

Try to read a newspaper article every day, either in print form or online. Use your local or school library to find other types of non-fiction texts, such as autobiographies.

Non-fiction texts: e.g. articles, reviews, speeches, journals, reference book extracts, autobiographies, letters, obituaries or travel writing.

21st

Extract from Who'd Be a Paper Boy? *Full text on page 105. Lines 15–18.*

You can have some sympathy for the kids. Standards in literacy and numeracy have fallen so steeply that it can be a real struggle identifying door names and numbers, and the Sunday papers are now so heavy that your averagely obese teenager just doesn't have the strength or stamina for the job.

Start to think about the writer's **purpose**, **tone** and **point of view.**

'kids' rather than 'children' suggests informal article?

Humour used to entertain as well as inform.

Sarcastic tone suggests author's view is that children are lazy.

Now try this

Read the next two paragraphs (lines 20–25) from *Who'd Be a Paper Boy?* by John Crace on page 105. Note down your ideas about purpose, audience and the writer's point of view.

Reading questions explained 1

You will need to answer certain **types of question** in the exam. The questions are based on extracts that you will not have seen before. The questions on this page are sample questions and do not need to be answered.

The skills you are tested on in these questions are called **assessment objectives**.

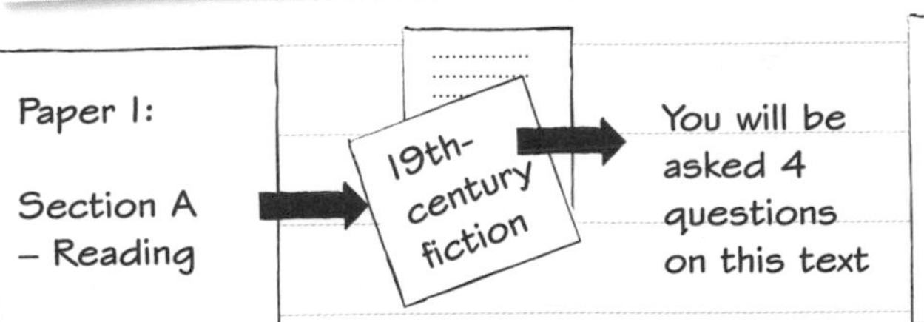
Paper 1:
Section A – Reading
19th-century fiction
You will be asked 4 questions on this text

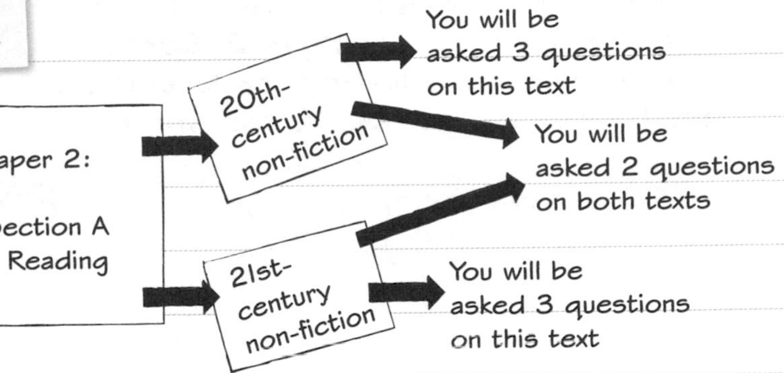
Paper 2:
Section A – Reading
20th-century non-fiction
21st-century non-fiction
You will be asked 3 questions on this text
You will be asked 2 questions on both texts
You will be asked 3 questions on this text

Assessment objective 1

Assessment objective 1 tests your ability to **identify and explain** the information in a text.

These are examples of the types of question that will be used to test this skill. The first question is a question from Paper 1 and the second from Paper 2.

1 In lines 1–6, identify the phrase that explains why the narrator thought she could get home before the snow started. **(1 mark)**

1 In lines 18–27, identify two reasons why the 'appearance' is terrifying for new cab drivers. **(2 marks)**

To revise these question types, turn to pages 10 and 11

In **Paper 2, assessment objective 1** will also be used to test your ability to **select information from two texts**. You will need to show your understanding by writing about both texts in your answer.

Refer to both texts in your answer.

7 (a) The two texts are both about foreign travel. What similarities are there between the writers' experiences of travelling abroad? Use evidence from both texts to support your answer. **(6 marks)**

To revise this question type, see pages 34–36

Assessment objective 2

Assessment objective 2 tests your ability to explain how writers use **language and structure to achieve effects.** You will need to try to use the **correct term** for the language or structural features in the text.

These are examples of the types of question that will be used to test this skill. The first question is a question from Paper 1 and the second from Paper 2.

3 In lines 9–22, how does the writer use language and structure to suggest the narrator's fear is increasing? Support your views with reference to the text. **(6 marks)**

3 Analyse how the writer uses language and structure to interest and engage readers. Support your views with detailed reference to the text. **(15 marks)**

To revise these question types, see pages 18–24

Now try this

What is the main difference between identifying information (assessment objective 1) and explaining how writers use language (assessment objective 2)?

Had a look ☐ Nearly there ☐ Nailed it! ☐

Reading questions explained 2

The questions on this page are sample questions and do not need to be answered.

Assessment objective 3

Assessment objective 3 tests your ability to **compare the views** put forward in the two non-fiction texts in **Paper 2: Section A – Reading**. You will also need to **compare the techniques** used by the two writers.

This is an example of the type of question that will be used to test this skill.

Refer to both texts in your answer.

7 (b) Compare how the writers of Text 1 and Text 2 present their ideas and perspectives about teenagers.
Support your answer with detailed reference to the texts. **(14 marks)**

To revise these question types, see pages 34–41

4 In this extract, there is an attempt to build tension.
Evaluate how successfully this is achieved.
Support your views with detailed reference to the text. **(15 marks)**

This is a Paper 1 question.

This is a Paper 2 question.

6 Bill Bryson attempts to entertain the reader through his description of hotels and guest houses.
Evaluate how successfully this is achieved.
Support your views with detailed reference to the text. **(15 marks)**

To revise these question types, see pages 42–46

These are examples of the type of question that will be used to test this skill.

Assessment objective 4

Assessment objective 4 tests your ability to evaluate texts. This means **explaining** the **ideas** and **point of view** expressed by the writer and forming a judgement about how successful you think the text is. You will need to use **appropriate quotations** to support your views. You can give your own opinion, but only if you back this up with a solid explanation that relates firmly to the text.

Getting it right

Read the questions carefully to see if you are told which lines of the text to focus on:

- If line numbers are given in the question, make sure you refer to the correct section of the text in your answer.
- If no line numbers are given, read the question again to see if there is a particular aspect of the text you need to concentrate on.

Now try this

Look back at the exam-style questions on this page. None of them give line numbers but they all ask you to look at a particular aspect of the text. Circle or highlight the words in each question that tell you what aspect of the text to focus on.

Reading the questions

You need to read each question on the exam paper very carefully to make sure you know exactly what it is asking you to do. Make sure you know how to focus on the **key words in questions**. The questions on this page are sample questions and do not need to be answered. Focus instead on picking out the key words and fully understanding the questions.

Paper 1

2 From lines 1–4, give **two** reasons why the narrator's childhood was difficult.
You may use your own words or quotation from the text. **(2 marks)**

Check which lines you are being asked to write about.

Identify how many pieces of information you are being asked to find.

Don't explain here. You are only being asked to find and list the reasons.

You can quote from the text or use your own words.

Paper 1

3 In lines 4–12, how does the writer use language and structure to show the narrator's anger?
Support your views with reference to the text. **(6 marks)**

Make sure you write about both language and structure.

You must explain **how** the writer achieves effects.

Pick out the key words in the question that tell you which aspect of the text to focus on. Make sure you use them in your answer.

Use quotations to support your explanations.

Paper 2

6 John Crace attempts to entertain the reader with his views about teenagers.
Evaluate how successfully this is achieved.
Support your views with detailed reference to the text. **(15 marks)**

No line numbers are given, so you need to use the whole extract for your answer.

Check if you should write about the whole text or just one specific aspect of it.

Ensure you make and explain a judgement about how well the text achieves its aims.

Here, you will need to make sure you use quotations for every point that you make.

Now try this

Look at the exam-style question opposite.

1. How many texts should you write about?
2. Does this question require you to consider the whole of each text or just particular sections?
3. What are the key words in the question?
4. How long should you spend on this question?

Refer to both texts in your answer.

7 (b) Compare how the writers of Text 1 and Text 2 present their ideas and perspectives about foreign travel.
Support your answer with detailed reference to the texts. **(14 marks)**

This is a Paper 2 question.

Had a look ☐ Nearly there ☐ Nailed it! ☐

Skimming for the main idea or theme

Maximise the time available in the exam by **skim reading**. First, skim the texts for their main idea or theme. Then follow up with a second, more detailed reading. In particular, skimming will help you with the **non-fiction** extracts in **Paper 2**.

Key features

Look at these key places when you skim read a text.

The heading.

The first sentence of each paragraph.

The last sentence of the text.

21st

Who'd Be a Paper Boy?

It's cold, it's dark and you've got to bolt your breakfast before dragging a bag full of papers round the streets. To add insult to injury, you then have to go to school. So who would be bothered with a paper round? Almost no one these days, it seems…

New research from the Cartoon Network shows that your average kid is raking in £770 a year, of which only £32 comes from paper rounds. Which rather suggests that most teenagers last only about a week and a half in the job before finding it a bit much…

And if the little darlings can't stretch to a please and thank you, they can always flog a few household items on eBay. Failing that, there's always the tooth fairy.

Summing up

Think about how you could sum up the text in one or two sentences.
Here are some ideas for the text on the right:

Modern teenagers are not interested in paper rounds.

The teenagers of today are lazy and have easier ways of making money than paper rounds.

Getting it right

To make your skim reading even more useful, read the **questions** carefully first. The questions will give you clues about the **main ideas or themes** in the texts.

Remember to look at:
- the heading
- the first sentence of each paragraph
- the last sentence of the text.

Now try this

Give yourself 30 seconds to skim read the article *The History of London's Black Cabs* by Ian Beetlestone on page 104. Can you sum up the main idea or theme in one, or at most two sentences?

Annotating the texts

For **both papers**, get into the habit of **highlighting, underlining or circling** parts of a text that you can use to support your answers. Then write a note to yourself about why it will be useful in supporting your response. This is called **annotating**.

Annotating

Have a look at this question and the annotated extract below.

3 In lines 21–24, how does the writer use language and structure to suggest conditions in the prison are harsh? Support your views with reference to the text. **(6 marks)**

This is a Paper 1 question.

Getting ready to annotate

Before you start annotating:

- check which lines you need to write about
- pick out the key words in the question – this will keep your annotations focused.

Gathering information for your answer

You can gather information for your answer to a Paper 1 exam-style question like the one above by annotating the text like this:

19th

Extract from Little Dorrit. *Full text on page 96. Lines 21–24.*

As the captive men were faded and haggard, so the iron was rusty, the stone was slimy, the wood was rotten, the air was faint, the light was dim. Like a well, like a vault, like a tomb, the prison had no knowledge of the brightness outside, and would have kept its polluted atmosphere intact in one of the spice islands of the Indian ocean.

Emotive language for description – shows effect of prison on men

List of negative descriptions

Similes – suggest men will literally die in the prison

Adjective – suggests prison is poisonous and emphasises harm to men's health

Getting it right

Do not just highlight useful quotations. For each highlight, note down:

- the effect on the reader
- the technique used to achieve it.

Try to use the correct technical language if you know it.

Now try this

Read another extract from *Little Dorrit*, opposite. Highlight, underline or circle any words or phrases that you think you could use to answer the exam-style question at the top of this page.

Remember to make a note of the effect that each highlighted word or phrase has on the reader, and the technique that is used to achieve that effect.

19th

Extract from Little Dorrit. *Full text on page 96. Lines 9–12.*

Besides the two men, a notched and disfigured bench, immovable from the wall, with a draught-board rudely hacked upon it with a knife, a set of draughts, made of old buttons and soup bones, a set of dominoes, two mats, and two or three wine bottles. That was all the chamber held, exclusive of rats and other unseen vermin, in addition to the seen vermin, the two men.

Putting it into practice

In **Paper 1: Section A – Reading**, you'll need to respond to how writers use **language for effect** in a **prose fiction** text from the **19th century**. Read the extract from *The Adventures of Tom Sawyer* by Mark Twain on page 98. Then read the exam-style question below and look at how a student has used annotation to help them respond to it.

Here we are focusing on language, but in the exam you will need to comment on structure for this type of question, too.

Worked example

3 In lines 27–35, how does the writer use language and structure to suggest the children are losing hope?

Support your views with reference to the text.

(6 marks)

The verb 'fastened' suggests that the children literally cling on to the candle as if it is their last hope of finding their way out. The writer then personifies the candle using the verbs 'climb' and 'linger' to suggest that the situation has slipped out of the children's control. This lack of control is strengthened by the use of the word 'reigned', which suggests that the darkness has actually taken charge of the children. The darkness could also be seen as a metaphor for the loss of the children's hope of a rescue.

Note how these annotations lead to a focused, detailed response to the question. Take the time to annotate the fiction text to help you write a strong answer.

Commenting on language

For a question like this you should:

- ✓ spend about 12 minutes on your answer
- ✓ highlight key words in the question so that you get the focus right
- ✓ use only the lines of text referred to in the question
- ✓ focus on the way the writer has used words and sentences to create ideas about the narrator in the mind of the reader.

These are the sections of the text that the student highlighted, and the student's annotations.

> The children fastened their eyes upon their bit of candle …

Verb 'fastened' suggests they are desperate; they know the candle is their last hope of light

> … saw the half inch of wick stand alone at last; saw the feeble flame rise and fall, climb the thin column of smoke, linger …

Personification of candle emphasises that time is running out; verbs 'climb' and 'linger' also draw out the tension

> … the horror of utter darkness reigned!

'Reigned' suggests darkness has taken charge of the children; darkness as metaphor?

Now try this

Complete the 'Sample answer extract' above. Aim to identify at least **two** more relevant points.

Putting it into practice

In **Paper 2: Section A – Reading**, you'll need to respond to how writers use **language for effect** in **non-fiction** texts from the **20th and 21st centuries**. Read the extract from *Angela's Ashes* by Frank McCourt on page 100. Then read the exam-style question below and look at how a student has used annotation to help them respond to it.

Evaluating and referring to a text

For a question like this you should:

- spend about 15 minutes on your answer
- highlight key words in the question to help you keep your answer relevant
- refer to the whole text
- focus on the ideas and points of view expressed by the writer, and make a judgement about how successful you think the text is
- include a reference to the text for each point you make.

For more about using evidence, see page 14

Worked example

6 Frank McCourt attempts to engage the reader by describing how poorly prepared he was for his first job.
Evaluate how successfully this is achieved.
Support your views with detailed reference to the text. **(15 marks)**

McCourt successfully attempts to engage the reader by showing how he was laughed at and mocked when he started work. For instance, he was met by 'cackles' and jokes about cleaning the toilets, which makes the reader sympathise with him. He also writes that his mother 'brought a note', which suggests he is too young to get a job on his own. McCourt then goes on to describe how he was told to 'go away and wash', which suggests that he had not thought about how to present himself for work. He is also so poorly prepared that the women are very dismissive of him, as they refer to him rudely as a 'specimen'.

Note how this student answer extract uses key words from the question. Each point includes a reference from the text and is fully explained.

These are the sections of the text that the student highlighted, and the student's annotations.

The thin one cackles, Oh, God, I thought you were here to clean the lavatories.

The women laugh and mock – do not take him seriously as a telegram boy

My mother brought a note …

Suggests he is far too young for work

Go away and wash yourself …

He has not thought about how to present himself for a job

… who dragged in that specimen?

Women are dismissive of him, they don't think he is the right type for the job

Now try this

Complete the 'Sample answer extract' above. Aim to identify at least **three** more relevant points.

Remember to:

- focus on the key words in the question
- make your annotations detailed enough to use in your answer.

Had a look ☐ Nearly there ☐ Nailed it! ☐

Explicit information and ideas

In the reading sections of **both papers** you will be tested on whether you fully understand the writer's **main topic or theme**. You will need to respond to short questions that ask you to identify **explicit** information and ideas.

Looking for explicit information and ideas

Looking for explicit information and ideas means you will not be required to look for hidden meanings. You don't need to explain what you find. You will just need to find short quotations or paraphrase (put into your own words) what is clearly there.

explicit *adjective*

1. Stated clearly and in detail, leaving no room for confusion or doubt

'the arrangement had not been made explicit'

Synonyms: clear, direct, plain, obvious, straightforward, clear-cut, crystal clear, clearly expressed, easily understandable, blunt

This Paper 1 exam-style question is about *The Half-Brothers.*

19th

Extract from The Half-Brothers. *Full text on page 99. Lines 1–6.*

It looked dark and gloomy enough; but everything was so still that I thought I should have plenty of time to get home before the snow came down. Off I set at a pretty quick pace. But night came on quicker. The right path was clear enough in the day-time, although at several points two or three exactly similar diverged from the same place; but when there was a good light, the traveller was guided by the sight of distant objects,—a piece of rock,—a fall in the ground—which were quite invisible to me now.

Worked example

1 From lines 1–6, identify the phrase that explains why the narrator thought he could get home before the snow started. **(1 mark)**

everything was so still

This type of question is asking you to find 'explicit' (clear or obvious) information. Look at the extract on the right to see that it will only have one possible answer.

This Paper 2 exam-style question is about *Notes from a Small, Island* full text on page 103.

Worked example

4 What was the weather like when Bryson arrived in England? **(1 mark)**

Foggy ✓

The weather was foggy ✗

The text says 'My first sight of England was on a foggy March night.' ✗

For the 1-mark questions on **both papers**, keep your answers as brief as possible – you don't need to waste time writing in full sentences.

Now try this

You will need to look at *Who'd Be a Paper Boy?* on page 105 to answer these 1-mark questions.

1 How long ago was a paper round worth doing?
2 How much money does an average child get per year?
3 Which TV company has researched children's pocket money?

Implicit ideas

There will be questions on **both papers** that require you to identify both **explicit and implicit** information and ideas.

implicit *adjective*
1. Suggested though not directly expressed
'comments seen as implicit criticism of the children'
Synonyms: implied, indirect, inferred, understood, hinted, suggested, deducible

Reading between the lines

Writers do not always state their meaning explicitly. Sometimes you will have to work out what the writer is **suggesting** or **implying** – in other words, what is **implicit** in the text. This is sometimes called **making an inference** and is also referred to as **reading between the lines**.

Using inference to find implicit meaning

Look at how inference has been used here to come up with ideas about the narrator's childhood.

19th

Extract from Samuel Lowgood's Revenge. *Full text on page 97. Lines 2–4.*

I had been reared in a workhouse, had picked up chance waifs and strays of education from the hardest masters, and had been drafted, at the age of ten, into the offices of Tyndale and Tyndale.

- Suggests he had a hard childhood
- He had to fight for his education
- He had no choice but to start work at a very young age

21st

Extract from The History of London's Black Cabs. *Full text on page 104. Lines 10–14.*

The average "Knowledge Boy" (or, occasionally, Girl) spends three or four years covering around 20,000 miles within a six-mile radius of Charing Cross, out on their moped come rain, freezing wind, or traffic chaos. Hundreds of hours are spent drawing lines on laminated maps of the city, working out the most direct route from hotel to station, restaurant to office, monument to square.

This Paper 2 exam-style question is about *The History of London's Black Cabs*.

Worked example

1 In lines 10–14, identify **two** reasons why getting a cab licence is difficult. **(2 marks)**

1 Trainees have to cover a lot of miles. (Explicit)
2 Trainees have to be very tough and determined. (Implicit)

For the second point in this answer, inference has been used to work out that trainees would need to be tough as they have to go out in all weathers and all road conditions, as well as spending long hours working on their maps.

Now try this

Read the full extract from *The History of London's Black Cabs* by Ian Beetlestone on page 104. Find **four** more reasons why getting a cab licence is difficult.

Try to keep your answers very brief. Remember that short questions on explicit and implicit information are only worth one mark for each point you make. Exact quotations are not always necessary. You can paraphrase (put into your own words), too.

Had a look ☐ Nearly there ☐ Nailed it! ☐

Inference

In **both papers**, you will need to make **inferences** (read between the lines) when a question asks you about the feelings, thoughts, views and actions of the writer, or the people or places they are writing about. Remember, inference is about working out what the writer is **implying** (suggesting).

What is the writer implying here?

Tom is thinking ahead and making food last, but Becky is less practical

Becky is trying to be brave

Tom is more practical, he is thinking of the future

Becky is very frightened and can't be comforted

19th

Extract from The Adventures of Tom Sawyer. *Full text on page 98. Lines 6–12.*

Tom divided the cake and Becky ate with good appetite, while Tom nibbled at his moiety. There was abundance of cold water to finish the feast with. By-and-by Becky suggested that they move on again. Tom was silent a moment. Then he said:

"Becky, can you bear it if I tell you something?"

Becky's face paled, but she thought she could.

"Well, then, Becky, we must stay here, where there's water to drink. That little piece is our last candle!"

Becky gave loose to tears and wailings. Tom did what he could to comfort her, but with little effect.

This Paper 1 exam-style question is about *The Adventures of Tom Sawyer*.

Worked example

4 In this extract, Becky and Tom are shown to have different reactions to being trapped in the cave.
Evaluate how successfully this difference is shown.
Support your views with detailed reference to the text. **(15 marks)**

Tom is shown as someone who can think practically at the start of the extract as you are told he 'divided the cake' and 'nibbled', suggesting he is trying to make the food last. He is also presented as thinking ahead when he tells Becky that they should stay 'where there's water'. Becky, however, seems unable to think ahead, as she 'ate with good appetite', which suggests she gobbles the cake without thinking.

Look out for instructions like this. This means your answer needs to include references to or quotations from the text. You can see examples of this in the answer extract opposite.

A fully developed answer should:
- refer to evidence from the extract
- comment on what can be inferred from this evidence
- develop and summarise the point with further comments or additional information from the text
- evaluate (make and explain a judgement) about how well the text achieves its aims.

Use **short quotations** where possible, or paraphrase the text. This makes your inference really clear and specific.

Find out more about using quotations on page 14 and evaluating a text on pages 42–46

Now try this

Read lines 12–26 of the extract from *The Adventures of Tom Sawyer* by Mark Twain on page 98. Continue the 'Worked example answer' above using **three** short quotations from the new lines.

Remember to keep Question 4 above in mind. Choose quotations that clearly support the inferences you make.

Interpreting information and ideas

In **both papers** you will need to **interpret** the information, ideas and themes in a text. In **Paper 1: Section A – Reading**, the **fiction** text will be from the **19th century**. In **Paper 2: Section A – Reading**, one of the **non-fiction** texts may be from the **early 20th century**. Some of the words or phrases in older texts may be unfamiliar and tricky to interpret. You need to be able to infer the meaning and explain it in your own words.

Remember to look at the marks allocated to each question. Some questions that ask you to interpret information and ideas may only be worth one or two marks. For those, you only need to give brief answers.

Understanding unfamiliar words and phrases

When you are asked to explain an unfamiliar word or phrase, read the text **before** and **after** it in the extract. This will give you more information and help you to infer the meaning. Remember that you can use this approach with all kinds of text, not just the more challenging 19th-century ones.

Extract from Samuel Lowgood's Revenge. *Full text on page 97. Lines 1–4.*

I, too, was an orphan; but I was doubly an orphan. My father and mother had both died in my infancy. I had been reared in a workhouse, had picked up chance waifs and strays of education from the hardest masters, and had been drafted, at the age of ten, into the offices of Tyndale and Tyndale.

The phrase 'waifs and strays' describes his education and follows the words 'picked up' and 'chance'. This suggests that his education has been disorganised and not very thorough. Here, 'waifs and strays' is likely to mean unconnected bits and pieces.

Extract from Notes from a Small Island. *Full text on page 103. Lines 24–26.*

I hesitated in the shadows, feeling like a street urchin. I was socially and sartorially ill-suited for such an establishment and anyway it was clearly beyond my meagre budget.

Look at the sentence before. The word 'sartorially' is preceded by the phrase 'like a street urchin', which suggests Bryson is scruffily dressed.

Worked example

2 Give **one** example from lines 24–26 of how the writer uses language to show that Bryson does not feel able to enter the Churchill hotel.
Support your example with a detailed text reference.

(2 marks)

The phrase 'socially and sartorially ill-suited' suggests he feels awkward as he is unsuitably dressed.

This is a good answer to a Paper 2 question because it uses a quotation. The student has used inference to work out that 'sartorially' means something to do with Bryson's clothes.

Now try this

The following phrases are from the extract from *Samuel Lowgood's Revenge* on page 97. What do they mean?

- 'office drudge' (line 4)
- 'troublesome ladder' (line 5)
- 'pauper orphan' (line 7)

Getting it right

Remember:

- Read the text before and after unfamiliar words or phrases – this will help you to infer the meaning.
- Keep your answers brief – these questions are only worth one or two marks.

Had a look ☐ Nearly there ☐ Nailed it! ☐

Using evidence

For **both papers**, you need to use carefully chosen, **relevant evidence** to support the **points** you make in your answers. Quotations can be long or short, but you must use them correctly in your answer to obtain maximum marks.

Longer quotations: what to do

1. Introduce longer quotations with a colon.

2. Start the quotation on a new line.

3. Put your quotation in quotation marks.

4. Copy your quotation accurately.

5. Start your explanation on a new line.

The writer uses alliteration and a personal pronoun in his opening paragraph:

'To add insult to injury, you then have to go to school.'

This helps to engage readers by creating a sarcastic tone that mocks modern teenagers, and sets out the writer's view that they are lazy.

Shorter quotations can be more effective than longer ones. They:

- show you can identify key words and phrases
- allow you to focus on the writer's specific language choices.

Shorter quotations: what to do

1. You do not need to introduce each quotation with a colon or start a new line.
2. Put each quotation into quotation marks.
3. Make sure the sentence containing the embedded quotation makes sense.
4. Choose single-word quotations very carefully to ensure you can make an effective comment on them.

The writer uses negative adjectives such as 'sullen' and 'resentful' to describe the way mothers feel that their teenagers behave. These words emphasise the lack of understanding that exists between parents and teenagers as they exaggerate the negative aspects of teenage behaviour.

Embedding quotations means that you can use more than one quotation in a sentence to fully evidence your points.

Paraphrasing the text

Sometimes, like in the example below, you can refer closely to the text by turning it into your own words. This is called **paraphrasing**.

21st

Extract from Who'd Be a Paper Boy? *Full text on page 105. Lines 12–13.*

"I had four boys earning £20 a week for delivering about 18 papers each per day, and every day at least one would fail to turn up …"

The shop owner feels that teenagers are not reliable enough to employ, despite the fact that paper rounds appear to be reasonably well paid.

Remember: paraphrasing is effective when evaluating the whole text but use short quotations when you answer questions on language.

Now try this

1 The following quotations are from *Notes from a Grandmother* on page 101. Embed them in two sentences explaining what parents should avoid when dealing with teenage children.
- 'blind eye' (line 21)
- 'confrontation' (line 23)

2 Now read lines 23–25 from the text. Explain how the writer suggests parents should deal with their difficult teenage children.

Point – Evidence – Explain

P-E-E is a technique you can use in your longer answers for **Paper 2** to make them clearer and better organised.

1. Make your **point**.
2. Provide **evidence** to support the point.
3. **Explain** how the evidence supports the point.

Getting it right

P-E-E is particularly useful when answering questions that ask you to:
- **comment** on language and structure
- **evaluate** a text
- **compare** texts.

P-E-E in practice

You should use a range of phrases to link your point, evidence and **explanation**.

1. Make your point: The writer uses | The article focuses on
2. Introduce your evidence: For example, | The writer describes | For instance,
3. Introduce your explanation: This gives the impression that | The writer is implying that | This suggests | This shows

Worked example

3 Analyse how the writer uses language and structure to interest and engage readers. Support your views with detailed reference to the text. **(15 marks)**

The writer mixes serious points with humour. For instance, his point about standards falling 'steeply' is serious but then he jokes that this means teenagers cannot even identify 'door names and numbers'. By making a serious point in an entertaining way, the writer is able to engage as well as inform readers.

- The paragraph opens with a detailed point that addresses the question.
- The adverbial 'for instance' shows clearly that evidence will be used and two quotations are given.
- Short quotations are effectively embedded within the sentence.
- The evidence is then explained in detail with a comment on the effect of the language on the reader.

You can improve your P-E-E paragraphs by using more than one piece of evidence to back up a more fully developed point.

21st

Extract from Who'd Be a Paper Boy? *Full text on page 105. Lines 15–18.*

You can have some sympathy for the kids. Standards in literacy and numeracy have fallen so steeply that it can be a real struggle identifying door names and numbers.

Now try this

Read the extract from *Who'd Be a Paper Boy?* Full text on page 105. Lines 1–2 .
Choose a short quotation to support the following point: 'The writer uses negative language to make paper rounds seem unappealing.'

21st

It's cold, it's dark and you've got to bolt your breakfast before dragging a bag full of papers round the streets. To add insult to injury, you then have to go to school.

Had a look ☐ Nearly there ☐ Nailed it! ☐

Putting it into practice

In **Paper 1: Section A – Reading**, you'll need to respond to how a writer uses **language and structure** to achieve particular **effects**. Read the extract from *The Half-Brothers* by Elizabeth Gaskell on page 99. Then look at the exam-style question below and read the extracts from two students' answers.

Worked example

3 In lines 12–19, how does the writer use language and structure to suggest the narrator is becoming frightened?
Support your views with references to the text.
(6 marks)

Remember to read the question and skim read the text first. Then read the text again in more detail, and annotate it with your ideas.

Commenting on language and structure

For a question like this you should:

- spend about 12 minutes on your answer
- read the question carefully and **highlight the main focus**
- only use the lines of text **referred to in the question**
- comment on **how** the writer uses language and structure and what the **effects** are on the reader.

Sample answer extract

The word 'suddenly' suggests the weather changes quickly so there was nothing the narrator could do. The narrator is also becoming frightened as he loses all sense of direction and is surrounded by 'darkness'.

✗ Although a quotation is used, there is no clear point and the explanation is just a definition of the word 'suddenly' rather than a comment on its effect.

✗ This refers back to the question but does not develop the explanation by explaining the effects.

You should use P-E-E to help you structure your answer so that it includes a clear explanation of how your evidence supports your point.

Improved sample answer

The writer suggests the narrator is becoming frightened by creating a sense of tension. For instance, the word 'suddenly' suggests a change in mood and the phrase 'filled thick with dusky flakes' creates a vivid picture in the reader's mind of how frightened the narrator would be by the blinding snow.

✓ Clear point that refers directly to the question.

✓ Use of the adverbial 'for instance' signals clear use of relevant quotations, which are embedded within the sentence.

✓ A fully developed explanation that refers back to the question.

Note how this answer refers directly to the effect of the writer's choices on the reader.

Now try this

Complete the 'Improved sample answer' above.
Aim to identify and explain **two** more relevant points.

Use a clear P-E-E structure to make your answer clear and focused on the question.

Putting it into practice

In **Paper 2: Section A – Reading**, you'll need to respond to how a writer uses **language and structure** for **effect**. Read the extract from *The History of London's Black Cabs* by Ian Beetlestone on page 104. Then look at the exam-style question below and read the extracts from two students' answers.

Worked example

3 Analyse how the writer uses language and structure to interest and engage readers. Support your views with detailed reference to the text. **(15 marks)**

Commenting on language and structure

For a question like this you should:

- ✓ spend about 15 minutes on your answer
- ✓ read the question carefully and **highlight the main focus**
- ✓ refer to the **whole text** as no line numbers are given
- ✓ comment on **how** the writer uses language and structure and what the **effects** are on the reader.

Sample answer extract

The writer engages the reader by showing that working as a London cab driver is difficult, as the writer can't even open the doors to start with, and panics when two passengers get into his cab.

He also doesn't know where to go as his nerves are 'frayed'.

✓ Clear introduction that refers to the question, although the explanation is not really clear at the end of the sentence.

✗ This section only gives evidence without making a point or explaining the effect of the writer's use of language.

Remember that P-E-E stands for **Point – Evidence – Explain.** You need to include an explanation to make your answer complete and effective.

Improved sample answer

The writer engages the reader's interest by showing that working as a London cab driver is difficult as the writer can't even open the doors to start with, and he panics when he gets his first two passengers. This suggests that it is a nerve-racking job that probably requires proper training. The writer then goes on to say that his nerves are 'frayed', and he makes a joke by calling the destination 'Tuxedo Junction'. This suggests that the job of a cab driver is difficult, as it has made him very nervous and unable even to think about the correct route.

✓ Clear introduction that refers to the question, followed by clear evidence from the text.

✓ Use of the pronoun 'This' links the two sentences and clearly signals an explanation.

✓ Further examples are provided of the writer's choice of language and tone.

✓ Clear and fully developed explanation that links back to the question.

Now try this

Complete the 'Improved sample answer'. Aim to identify and explain **three** more relevant points and focus on using a clear P-E-E structure for your answers.

Remember to:

- make a clear point
- use evidence from the text to support your point
- explain how the evidence you use supports your point.

Word classes

In **both papers** you will be asked to comment on the writers' **choice of language**. Start by thinking about the types of words – or **word classes** – writers use.

Nouns

These are words used to describe:

- objects: e.g. bag, door, bottle
- people: e.g. man, traveller, Frank
- places: e.g. London, counting-house, Covent Garden
- ideas: e.g. hunger, sympathy, keenness.

Verbs

These are words used to describe:

- actions: e.g. to drag, to wander, to trip
- occurrences: e.g. to arrive, to survive
- states: e.g. to be, to think, to dream.

Remember: **pronouns** such as 'he', 'they', 'it' can replace or stand in for **nouns**.

Adjectives

These are words to describe a noun: e.g. foggy, elegant, clear, cold, dark.

Remember: **adjectives** can become **comparatives** (e.g. 'longer', 'darker') and **superlatives** (e.g. 'longest', 'darkest).

Adverbs

These words qualify verbs. They are usually formed by adding 'ly' to an adjective (but not always) – e.g. abruptly, immediately, slowly, instantly, often, sometimes.

Adverbs can also modify adjectives and other adverbs.

Getting it right

Make sure you are familiar with these adjective forms and how to use them.

- **Comparatives** give degrees of difference: e.g. clearer, colder, darker, more elegant.
- **Superlatives** identify the most or least: e.g. clearest, coldest, darkest, most elegant.

Examples

Here are some sample student comments about the extracts opposite, focusing on word class:

1 … I was panicking, pressing all the buttons I could find, fumbling with keys.

The writer uses the verbs 'panicking', 'pressing' and 'fumbling' to focus the reader's mind on his nerves and lack of skill.

2 And if the little darlings can't stretch to a please and thank you, they can always flog a few household items on eBay.

The writer uses the noun 'darlings' rather than children as he is being sarcastic about how spoilt teenagers are today.

3 As the captive men were faded and haggard, so the iron was rusty, the stone was slimy, the wood was rotten, the air was faint, the light was dim.

The writer uses strong adjectives to create a vivid picture.

Now try this

Read lines 8–12 of the extract from *Samuel Lowgood's Revenge* by Mary E. Braddon on page 97. Write **two** sentences commenting on the writer's choice of language and its effect. Focus on word class. How has the writer used nouns, verbs, adjectives and adverbs, as well as any comparatives or superlatives, for effect?

Connotations

Some words can create bigger ideas in our minds through the ideas and attitudes they suggest. These ideas and attitudes are called **connotations**.

Thinking about what a word or phrase suggests can help you to write effective comments on the writer's choice of language in **both papers**. Look at what the phrase 'white-hot arrow' could suggest in the example opposite.

Extract from Little Dorrit. *Full text on page 96. Line 2.*

... it shot in like a white-hot arrow.

The connotations of the phrase 'white-hot arrow' suggest the sun can actually pierce and wound. This, in turn, emphasises the heat of the day and makes it seem deadly.

Language choice

These sentences have similar literal meanings, but the connotations of the nouns and verbs that have been used let you know the writer's **real attitude**.

The ground moved under me.

The mud shifted under me.

The boggy soil quaked under me.

Connotations in context

Words can have different meanings depending on what comes before or after them in a text. You need to think about what comes **before** and **after** – the context – to interpret words correctly and understand their connotations.

context *noun*
The parts of something written or spoken that immediately precede and follow a word or passage and clarify its meaning.

Exploring the **connotations** of the language in a text can help you to write about the **atmosphere** that is created, or about the **attitude** of the writer.

Extract from Samuel Lowgood's Revenge. *Full text on page 97. Lines 2–4.*

I had been reared in a workhouse, had picked up chance waifs and strays of education from the hardest masters, and had been drafted, at the age of ten, into the offices of Tyndale and Tyndale.

This literally means raised or brought up but here it has connotations of rearing animals, and suggests he was treated harshly.

This is a phrase used to describe homeless people, and here it suggests that his education was patchy and perhaps unsuitable for a young child.

This literally means selected but here it has connotations of being forced, particularly as the sentence goes on to explain that he was only ten.

Now try this

Now read lines 8–34 of the extract from *Little Dorrit* by Charles Dickens on page 96. What are the connotations of these words and phrases?

hacked | taint | slimy | polluted | wild beast

Write **one** brief sentence to explain the literal meaning and the connotation of **each** word.

Figurative language

For **Paper 1** you will need to comment on the way writers use **language** to create **atmosphere** or to make readers feel a particular **emotion**. **Figurative language**, or **imagery**, is often used to create pictures in the reader's mind and make description more vivid.

Non-fiction texts use these techniques sometimes, too. Remember to look out for them in **Paper 2**.

Comment on figurative language

To improve your exam answers you will need to **explain** the **effect** of figurative language in a text.

Getting it right

When you are commenting on figurative language, make sure you:

- comment on the **effect** of the language used
- give the name for the **figurative device** used if you know it.

simile *noun*
A figure of speech involving the indirect comparison of one thing to another, usually using 'as' or 'like'

19th

Extract from Little Dorrit. *Full text on page 96. Lines 1–2.*

Grant it but a chink or a keyhole, and it shot in like a white-hot arrow.

Here the sun is likened to an arrow that can shoot through a keyhole. This emphasises the strength of the sun, and shows that there is very little escape from its searing heat.

metaphor *noun*
A direct comparison suggesting a resemblance between one thing and another

19th

Extract from Samuel Lowgood's Revenge. *Full text on page 97. Lines 4–5.*

Errand boy, light porter, office drudge, junior clerk – one by one I had mounted the rounds in this troublesome ladder, which for me could only be begun from the very bottom …

The writer uses a metaphor of a ladder to describe his difficult rise to the top of his profession. This metaphor makes his progression seem slow and difficult and it highlights the fact that he has had to stop and do every lowly job on the way.

Personification *noun*
Describing something non-human as if it were human

19th

Extract from The Half-Brothers. *Full text on page 99. Lines 13–15.*

It cut me off from the slightest knowledge of where I was, for I lost every idea of the direction from which I had come, so that I could not even retrace my steps; it hemmed me in, thicker, thicker, with a darkness that might be felt.

The writer personifies the snow to make it seem more dangerous, as if it is literally surrounding the narrator and preventing him from moving.

Now try this

Read the extract from *Little Dorrit* opposite. Identify the **two** figurative devices used, then write one or two sentences about the effect each example is intended to have on the reader.

Remember to name the figurative device used if you can.

Extract from Little Dorrit. *Full text on page 96. Lines 22–24.*

Like a well, like a vault, like a tomb, the prison had no knowledge of the brightness outside, and would have kept its polluted atmosphere intact in one of the spice islands of the Indian ocean.

Creation of character

For **Paper 1** you may need to comment on the way a writer has used **language** to create a particular **impression** of a **character**.

Character through action

Consider what the character **does** in the extract.

The adverb 'instantly' shows Tom to be alert and suggests he has taken charge, as does the verb 'leading', which also suggests he is the braver of the two children. He also seems sensible as he stops to listen again.

Extract from The Adventures of Tom Sawyer. *Full text on page 98. Lines 40–42.*

There was a sound like the faintest, far-off shout. Instantly Tom answered it, and leading Becky by the hand, started groping down the corridor in its direction. Presently he listened again; again the sound was heard, and apparently a little nearer.

Look out for **action** words – **verbs** and **adverbs**.

Extract from Little Dorrit. *Full text on page 96. Lines 34–37.*

… he was large and tall in frame, had thin lips, where his thick moustache showed them at all, and a quantity of dry hair, of no definable colour, in its shaggy state, but shot with red. The hand with which he held the grating (seamed all over the back with ugly scratches newly healed), …

Look out for **describing words** (adjectives) and **figurative language**.

Character through description

Look at **how** the writer **describes** the character.

The writer uses adjectives to emphasise the size and power of the character. The adjective 'thin' for his lips has connotations of meanness and red hair has connotations of a fiery temper. This is also suggested by the 'ugly scratches' on his hands, which may have come from fighting.

Character through dialogue

Think about how **dialogue** is used to build up an idea of the character.

Tom is shown to be reassuring in his answers here, and his answer 'Well, Becky?' suggests he is staying calm. He also appears positive as he responds 'certainly they will' and 'I reckon maybe they are' to Becky's worries about whether anybody will look for them.

Extract from The Adventures of Tom Sawyer. *Full text on page 98. Lines 13–18.*

"Tom!"

"Well, Becky?"

"They'll miss us and hunt for us!"

"Yes, they will! Certainly they will!"

"Maybe they're hunting for us now, Tom."

"Why, I reckon maybe they are. I hope they are."

Look out for **colloquial** (informal or conversational) **language**.

Now try this

Read lines 1–22 in the extract from *The Adventures of Tom Sawyer* by Mark Twain on page 98. Identify **two** more examples of how dialogue is used to create character. Write a P-E-E paragraph for each example.

Use technical language where you can to strengthen your response.

Creating atmosphere

For **Paper 1** you will need to think about how writers use a wide range of **language devices** in order to create an **atmosphere**. Sometimes this is called the **'mood' or 'tone'** of a piece of writing. You may also be asked to comment on how a writer presents a **setting**.

Personification of prison – makes it sound menacing and dangerous

Sun is personified – 'obtrusive stare' to emphasise the heat but 'blinked at it' suggests the prison is so forbidding even the sun can't look at it for long

19th

Extract from Little Dorrit. *Full text on page 96. Lines 7–12.*

In Marseilles that day there was a villainous prison. In one of its chambers, so repulsive a place that even the obtrusive stare blinked at it, and left it to such refuse of reflected light as it could find for itself, were two men. … That was all the chamber held, exclusive of rats and other unseen vermin, in addition to the seen vermin, the two men.

Suggests there are creatures in the prison even worse than rats

Noun 'refuse' has connotations of rubbish and decay, suggests prison looks dirty and neglected

Taking an overview

When you have identified the language techniques used and their connotations and effects, look at whether the techniques work together to create a particular mood or tone. This is called taking an 'overview' and can help you to show the examiner that you fully understand the extract.

The overall tone of the extract above is one of danger and decay.

Getting it right

When you answer a question about language techniques, it is a good idea to start with your 'overview' to sum up the overall effect created by the writer. You can do this by using phrases like these:

Overall, the writer suggests…

Overall, the writer creates…

The overall tone of the extract is…

Now try this

Read lines 32–35 of the extract from *The Half-Brothers* by Elizabeth Gaskell on page 99. Annotate **three** examples of language that creates atmosphere. For each one, comment on its effect or connotations. Then take an 'overview'. What overall mood or tone is created by the writer?

Narrative voice

For **Paper 1: Section A – Reading**, you may need to discuss **narrative voice** in your response to a question. (On rare occasions you may also need to do this for narrative non-fiction in **Paper 2**.) Narrative voice is the 'voice' a writer of fiction chooses to tell the story. The choice of narrative voice can be used to create a particular **point of view**.

First person narrative

This is a narrative written in the **first person**. The story is told by an **'I'**. The 'I' can be the main character or a less important character who is witnessing events. This point of view is effective in giving a sense of **closeness to the character** and readers are often encouraged to sympathise with them.

Extract from Samuel Lowgood's Revenge. *Full text on page 97. Lines 23–24.*

I hated him. I hated his foppish ways and his haughty manners; I hated his handsome boyish face, with its frame of golden hair, and its blue, beaming, hopeful eyes; I hated him …

Third person narrative

This is a narrative written in the **third person**. All characters are described using pronouns such as **'he'** and **'she'**, or by their **name**. In a third person narrative, the narrator is not a character in the story. Sometimes this type of narrator knows everything, including a character's thoughts; sometimes they only appear to look in from the outside.

19th

Extract from The Adventures of Tom Sawyer. *Full text on page 98. Lines 23–24.*

A frightened look in Becky's face brought Tom to his senses and he saw that he had made a blunder. Becky was not to have gone home that night! The children became silent and thoughtful.

In this extract, the third person narrative is all-knowing. This is called an omniscient narrator. An omniscient narrator knows the thoughts and feelings of all the characters in a narrative. This means the reader knows both children's thoughts and feelings. This is a deliberate way of making the reader sympathetic towards Tom.

This Paper 1 exam-style question is about *The Adventures of Tom Sawyer*. Full text on page 98.

Worked example

3 In lines 23–29, how does the writer use language and structure to suggest that Tom is brave?
Support your views with reference to the text. **(6 marks)**

The writer has used third person omniscient narration to show the reader what Tom is thinking. The phrase 'brought Tom to his senses' suggests he can be calm under pressure and is able to look after Becky, who is 'frightened' and therefore probably weaker than him. This may make the reader admire Tom, as they are both children, but he is able to think about somebody else when he is in danger.

✓ Clearly identifies the narrative voice.

✓ Interprets what the narrative voice tells the reader about the character's thoughts and suggests what this reveals about the character.

✓ Suggests the effect on the reader.

Now try this

Read lines 30–35 of the extract from *The Adventures of Tom Sawyer* by Mark Twain on page 98. Write one clear P-E-E paragraph commenting on the writer's use of third person narration and its effects.

Remember, using a P-E-E structure in your answer will help to make your answer clear, focused and fully developed.

Had a look ☐ Nearly there ☐ Nailed it! ☐

Putting it into practice

In **Paper 1: Section A – Reading**, you'll need to respond to the **language** in a **fiction** text. Read the extract from *The Half-Brothers* by Elizabeth Gaskell on page 99. Then look at the exam-style question below and read the extracts from two students' answers.

Worked example

3 In lines 27–35, how does the writer use language and structure to suggest that the narrator is becoming aware of a real danger? Support your views with reference to the text.

(6 marks)

Here the focus is on language but in the exam you will need to write about structure for this type of question, too.

Writing about language

For a question like this you should:

- ✓ spend about 12 minutes on your answer
- ✓ read the question carefully and highlight the main focus
- ✓ only use the lines of the text referred to in the question
- ✓ identify the language and structural techniques used and comment on their effects.

Use the technical names for language techniques where you can.

Sample answer extract

The writer uses the word 'visions' to suggest that the narrator is hallucinating, which suggests fear. The writer then uses the noun 'agony' to describe the narrator's feelings and the verb 'gathered' to show that he is still able to take action. Then the writer uses the three adjectives 'long, despairing, wailing', which suggest that the narrator is very frightened.

- ✗ No overview at the start of the answer.
- ✓ Some explanation is given that is related to the question.
- ✗ Identifies word classes but no clear point or reference to question.
- ✗ An explanation that includes comment about effect, but is not very detailed and has no reference to question.

An overview can still be used even if the question asks about the atmosphere of a text. Include an overview to show that you recognise the main techniques used by the writer.

Improved sample answer

Overall, the writer suggests that the narrator recognises the increasing danger by using a first person narrative voice, which allows the reader to know what the narrator is thinking and feeling. The narrator states that he had a 'vivid dream', which is like 'visions', and has connotations of hallucinations caused by extreme fear. This suggests that the narrator recognises an increase in danger. This is also suggested by the use of the verb 'gathered', as despite being in 'agony' – which suggests actual physical pain – the narrator recognises the need to take immediate action.

- ✓ Very clear overview at the start of the answer.
- ✓ Clear quotations and explanation that develop the point made in the overview.
- ✓ Clear identification of word classes and the word 'also' signal that more than one piece of evidence is being used to develop the point fully.

Note how the points made in this answer are well developed, and how the evidence from the text is clearly explained.

Now try this

Write another detailed P-E-E paragraph in answer to Paper 1 exam-style question 3 above.

Rhetorical devices 1

For **Paper 2** you will need to think about the range of **language** or **rhetorical devices** that writers use to **emphasise** their points or to **manipulate** the reader's response.

Extract from Who'd Be a Paper Boy? *Full text on page 105. Lines 1–5.*

It's cold, it's dark and you've got to bolt your breakfast before dragging a bag full of papers round the streets. To add insult to injury, you then have to go to school. So who would be bothered with a paper round? Almost no one these days, it seems.

The writer has put a list into a pattern of three to highlight and exaggerate the negative aspects of getting up to do a paper round.

pattern of three: a trio of words or phrases used to highlight or exaggerate a point for emphasis

list: series of items or ideas, often used to highlight quantity or variety

The writer has used alliteration to create humour and to emphasise how unappealing paper rounds are to young people.

alliteration: two or more words close to each other that begin with same sound; used for emphasis

Using a rhetorical question in the first paragraph engages the reader, as does the colloquialism 'bothered', and invites them to agree with the answer given.

rhetorical question: a question used to engage the reader but not necessarily expecting an answer

colloquialism: informal, conversational word or phrase

Getting it right

Remember to comment on the effect a device has, rather than just naming it. Use the technical name for the device if you know it, but even if you don't, you should still comment on the language and its effect.

Now try this

Read the whole of the extract from *Who'd Be a Paper Boy?* on page 105. Identify as many other examples of rhetorical devices as you can. Write **one** sentence about the effect **each** device is intended to have on the reader.

Remember, you can also identify and comment on the effects of the word classes and figurative language used!

For a reminder about word classes and figurative language see pages 18 and 20

Rhetorical devices 2

Here are some more rhetorical devices you need to be able to recognise and comment on.

Extract from The Hungry Cyclist. *Full text on page 102. Lines 2–8.*

Gasping for breath I said goodbye to a country I had fallen in love with and entered another. From the border, where the usual money changers, pickpockets and disgruntled border officials did everything to make life worse, I rode towards Quito. But in Ecuador it seemed as though someone had dimmed the lights and turned down the volume. Gone were the smiles and friendly cheers of encouragement from the roadside. Gone were the picturesque colonial farmsteads with their flower-covered porches. Here homes were functional, unfinished concrete, spewing construction steel. It rained, it was cold and I wanted to turn around.

The writer uses the verb 'gasping' to make the reader feel sympathy for the narrator, as it suggests he is struggling to breathe.

emotive language: words intended to create an extreme response or play on the reader's emotions

The writer repeatedly contrasts the attractive natural landscape he has left behind with the stark landscape of Ecuador in order to emphasise how unwelcome it appears.

contrast: comparing two opposing or different ideas to emphasise the difference between them

Repeating the word 'gone' emphasises the contrast between the two countries and exaggerates the negative aspects of Ecuador.

repetition: a repeated word or phrase to emphasise an idea

Extract from Who'd Be a Paper Boy? *Full text on page 105. Lines 15–19.*

You can have some sympathy for the kids. Standards in literacy and numeracy have fallen so steeply that it can be a real struggle identifying door names and numbers, and the Sunday papers are now so heavy that your averagely obese teenager just doesn't have the strength or stamina for the job. But the bottom line is that most kids can no longer be bothered to get out of bed for £20.

The writer uses hyperbole to emphasise the laziness of modern teenagers when it comes to earning money.

hyperbole: extreme exaggeration used to make a point

Getting it right

Make sure you are familiar with these rhetorical devices and how they can be used:

- pattern of three
- list
- alliteration
- rhetorical question
- colloquialism
- emotive language
- repetition
- contrast
- hyperbole

Now try this

Read the next paragraph (lines 9–15) of the extract from *The Hungry Cyclist* on page 102. Identify **two** other examples of rhetorical devices. Write **one** sentence about the way in which **each** device is used to manipulate the response of the reader.

Fact, opinion and expert evidence

For **Paper 2** you will need to think about how writers make their ideas more **persuasive** or **convincing** by supporting them with **facts, opinions and expert evidence**.

Getting it right

Referring to how the writer has used facts, opinions and expert evidence can improve your answers.

fact
Something that can be **proved** to be true.
Example: *'Manchester is a city in the United Kingdom.'*

opinion
An idea or viewpoint that the writer or speaker **believes** to be true.
Example: *'Manchester is the greatest city on earth.'*

expert evidence
Facts or opinions provided by an expert on the subject.
Example: *'Barry Chesham, a travel writer with over 30 years' experience, says: "Manchester is the greatest city on earth."'*

Read the extract on the right. In this article the writer:

- makes his viewpoint clear by giving his **opinion**
- refers to **expert evidence** to back up his opinion
- supports his opinion with more **facts and statistics**.

21st

Extract from Who'd Be a Paper Boy? *Full text on page 105. Lines 15–25.*

You can have some sympathy for the kids. Standards in literacy and numeracy have fallen so steeply that it can be a real struggle identifying door names and numbers, and the Sunday papers are now so heavy that your averagely obese teenager just doesn't have the strength or stamina for the job. But the bottom line is that most kids can no longer be bothered to get out of bed for £20.

New research from the Cartoon Network shows that your average kid is raking in £770 a year, of which only £32 comes from paper rounds. Which rather suggests that most teenagers last only about a week and a half in the job before finding it a bit much.

The bulk of the cash comes from pocket money (£186) and part-time work (£256) – selling fags outside the school gates, presumably – but the most telling items are for performance-related pay.

Now try this

Read the text extract *Who'd Be a Paper Boy?* on page 105. Note down **one** further **fact**, **one** further **opinion** and **one** further piece of **expert evidence** that the writer uses to support his viewpoint.

Make sure you know the difference between a fact, an opinion and expert evidence.

Had a look ☐ Nearly there ☐ Nailed it! ☐

Identifying sentence types

For **both papers** you will need to comment on the types of sentences a writer uses to **create effects** and **influence** the reader.

Single-clause sentences

Single-clauses sentences (sometimes called simple sentences) are made up of just **one clause** (a unit of information) and provide **one piece of information** about an event or action.

They contain a subject and **one verb**.

For example:

She gives me two shillings.

This is the verb.

Subordinate clauses

A **subordinate clause** does not make sense on its own. It is **dependent** on the main clause. For example:

This is the main clause.

The telegram boys laughed until he had gone.

This is the subordinate clause.

Note how two clauses can be joined with conjunctions such as **until**, **although** and **if**. In the above example, the conjunction is **until**.

Sometimes, the clauses in a multi-clause sentence can be swapped round.

For example:

Until he had gone, the telegram boys laughed.

Coordinate clauses

Clauses are **coordinate** if they are an **equal** pair – in other words, neither clause is dependent on the other. For example:

The boys were laughing and the women were unkind.

These clauses are linked as an equal pair.

Note how the two clauses are joined with conjunctions such as **and**, **but** and **or**. In this example, the conjunction is **and**.

Multi-clause sentences

Multi-clause sentences (sometimes called compound and complex sentences) are made up of **more than one clause**. They contain **two or more verbs**.

Minor sentences

These are grammatically incomplete because they do not contain a verb.

For example:

Telegram boy, miss.

No, miss.

Carbolic soap.

Now try this

What kind of sentences are these? How do you know?

1 Because the boys were laughing, his face turned red.

2 They went shopping and had tea.

3 He is a telegram boy.

4 Fourteen.

Commenting on sentence types

How writers **structure a sentence** can have just as much impact on the reader as the language they choose. This is true for both **fiction (Paper 1)** and **non-fiction (Paper 2)** texts.

Long sentences

A longer multi-clause sentence with several subordinate clauses can be used in many ways, for example to create tension or atmosphere, or for emphasis. This type of sentence is most commonly used in texts aimed at adults.

19th

Extract from The Half-Brothers. *Full text on page 99. Lines 22–26.*

Now and then, I stood still and shouted again; but my voice was getting choked with tears, as I thought of the desolate helpless death I was to die, and how little they at home, sitting round the warm, red, bright fire, wotted what was become of me,—and how my poor father would grieve for me—it would surely kill him—it would break his heart, poor old man!

This long, multi-clause sentence creates a tense mood as it highlights how desolate the narrator feels about dying. Each extra clause adds another layer to the feeling of misery and despair.

Short sentences

Short, single-clause sentences are associated with texts for children, but can also be used in texts aimed at adults to create drama or to mimic a character's thoughts.

Extract from Notes from a Small Island. *Full text on page 103. Lines 19–21.*

'We're shut.'

'Oh.' But what about my supper?

'Try the Churchill. On the front.'

These short sentences show how rudely Bryson is treated by the hotel owner. His response is just one word, to reflect his lack of belief that anybody could treat him so rudely.

Long and short sentences

Putting a short sentence after a long sentence can increase the dramatic effect. A final short sentence can also be used to sum up or to contrast the content of the longer sentence that comes before it.

Extract from Notes from a Small Island. *Full text on page 103. Lines 44–46.*

I used some woollen socks as mittens and put a pair of flannel boxer shorts on my head as a kind of desperate headwarmer, then sank heavily back onto the bench and waited patiently for death's sweet kiss. Instead, I fell asleep.

The long sentence is used to exaggerate how cold he is by listing all that he has to wear to keep warm, and ends by comically suggesting he is actually waiting for death. The final sentence is short as it is used to create further humour by showing that instead of dying, he just falls asleep.

Now try this

Read the first three sentences (lines 1–3) of the extract from *The Half-Brothers* by Elizabeth Gaskell on page 99. Write **one** or **two** sentences explaining the effect of the sentence types used by the writer.

Remember that you do not need to quote whole sentences in your answers. It is enough to refer to them like this: 'the use of a short sentence' or 'the effect of the long multi-clause sentence about…'.

Structure: non-fiction

The **overall structure** of non-fiction texts can be used by writers to create a **particular tone**, to **structure** a text for a particular **purpose** or to **manipulate** the reader's response. You will need to explore this for **Paper 2**.

Note that some narrative non-fiction can read almost like fiction. The opening (beginning), development (middle) and conclusion (ending) are important in fiction texts too.

Opening

The opening of any text needs to **engage** the attention of the reader. In a non-fiction text, the opening, or **introduction**, can be used to set the scene, like the example on the right.

20th

Extract from Notes from a Grandmother. *Full text on page 101. Lines 1–3.*

There is life after teenage. Hard to believe when you're facing a screaming virago or sullen, resentful stranger. You are now a fallen idol. From Mum! who could put everything right, you have become Mum! who understands nothing.

The strong opening statement reassures the audience of parents that the text will contain helpful advice. In the second sentence, the writer shows empathy for the reader by describing the teenage behaviour they might be facing, which further reassures them that the text will be worth reading.

Development

The main, middle section of a text needs to hold the reader's interest so that they keep reading. This is often achieved by **changing the tone** or by creating a **contrasting argument**, as in the example on the right. The middle section can also be used to **develop an argument** or to give a **more detailed explanation** of the main point.

21st

Extract from The Hungry Cyclist. *Full text on page 102. Lines 13–16.*

Not at all tempted by the usual suspects that made up the options in these small Ecuadorian towns, I began to wonder if my hunger could hold out until breakfast.

But hello! What's this?

Picks up the tone of the conclusion of this article.

The pair of short sentences in the middle of the text signals that the tone of the writing is about to change. It also creates an informal tone, which makes it feel like the writer is having a conversation with the reader.

Conclusion

Writers need to leave readers with a lasting impression. Ending styles can include: vivid images, warnings, a sudden twist in the tail, calls to action, positivity or a summary of the main points made.

21st

Extract from The History of London's Black Cabs. *Full text on page 104. Lines 44–46.*

In love with London and in a career rut, I saw an opportunity to become a working part of this magical town.

As my old teacher Dean puts it: "Let's stay the pride of the world's taxi drivers – why not?"

This article ends on a positive note with a quotation that sums up the writer's view of London taxi drivers as a skilled breed of people.

Picks up the purpose of the conclusion of this speech – to rally and inspire the audience.

Now try this

Read *Notes from a Grandmother* lines 26–30 on page 101. Then write a sentence explaining why the writer ends the article with a short paragraph.

Think about the structural choices the writer has made and what effects these choices have.

Structure: fiction

Structure is also important when commenting on a **fiction** text. Writers of **fiction** use a variety of **narrative structures** to achieve particular effects. You will need to explore this for **Paper 1**.

Foreshadowing

foreshadowing *noun*
An advance sign or warning of what is to come in the future. The author of a mystery novel might use foreshadowing in an early chapter of their book to give readers an inkling of an impending murder.

19th

Extract from The Half-Brothers. *Full text on page 99. Lines 1–6.*

It looked dark and gloomy enough; but everything was so still that I thought I should have plenty of time to get home before the snow came down. Off I set at a pretty quick pace. But night came on quicker. The right path was clear enough in the day-time, although at several points two or three exactly similar diverged from the same place; but when there was a good light, the traveller was guided by the sight of distant objects,–a piece of rock,–a fall in the ground–which were quite invisible to me now.

The fear faced by the narrator later in the extract is foreshadowed by the short sentence about night falling and by the description of the landmarks that have become invisible.

Use of closely described detail or action

Describing detail or action closely can suggest time dragging or it can focus a reader's mind on the event taking place, giving it a sense of great importance.

19th

Extract from The Adventures of Tom Sawyer. *Full text on page 98. Lines 46–49.*

Tom got down on his breast and reached as far down as he could. No bottom. They must stay there and wait until the searchers came. They listened; evidently the distant shoutings were growing more distant! a moment or two more and they had gone altogether. The heart-sinking misery of it! Tom whooped until he was hoarse, but it was of no use. He talked hopefully to Becky; but an age of anxious waiting passed and no sounds came again.

Here the children's actions are listed and described in detail in order to give a sense of how long they have been trapped and how desperate their situation has become. Closely describing Tom's actions also helps to show him as brave.

Repetition

Repetition can be used to stress the importance of a word or phrase, or to highlight an idea.

19th

Extract from Samuel Lowgood's Revenge. *Full text on page 97. Lines 23–29.*

I hated him. I hated his foppish ways and his haughty manners; I hated his handsome boyish face, with its frame of golden hair, and its blue, beaming, hopeful eyes; I hated him for the sword which swung across the stiff skirts … I hated him for all these; but most of all, I hated him for his influence over Lucy Malden.

Here, the word 'hated' is repeated and combined with a list structure to emphasise the strength of the narrator's feelings.

This paragraph uses a long sentence to emphasise the build-up of the narrator's negative feelings.

Now try this

Read lines 30–37 of the extract from *The Adventures of Tom Sawyer* by Mark Twain on page 98. Write **one** or **two** sentences commenting on the writer's use of structure and its effects.

Remember that beginnings, middles and endings are important in fiction texts too. Is there a 'cliffhanger' (a dramatic ending that leaves the reader in suspense)?

Had a look ☐ Nearly there ☐ Nailed it! ☐

Putting it into practice

In **Paper 1: Section A – Reading**, you'll need to respond to the **structure** in a **fiction** text. Read the extract from *Samuel Lowgood's Revenge* by Mary E. Braddon on page 97. Then look at the exam-style question below and read the extracts from two students' answers.

Worked example

3 In lines 4–12, how does the writer use language and structure to highlight the narrator's anger?
Support your views with reference to the text. **(6 marks)**

Here we are focusing on structure, but in the exam you will need to comment on language for this type of question, too.

Writing about language and structure

For a question like this you should:

- ✓ spend about 12 minutes on your answer
- ✓ read the question carefully and **highlight the main focus**
- ✓ only use the lines of the text **referred to in the question**
- ✓ identify the **language** and **structural techniques** used and comment on their **effects**.

Sample answer extract

The writer uses close description of detail to show how angry the narrator is about Christopher Weldon. A list of lowly jobs such as 'errand boy' and 'light porter' is used to show how hard the narrator has worked. The pronoun 'I' is repeated several times and a long sentence is used to highlight his anger.

✓ Clear opening point that refers to the focus of the question.

✗ Identification of structural technique with evidence, but the explanation does not relate to the question.

✗ Two different techniques are identified but the explanation does not address 'how' the effect is created.

Avoid making points that aren't supported by evidence or explained. Make sure the evidence you choose helps you to answer the main focus of the question.

Improved sample answer

The writer highlights the narrator's anger by closely describing details using repetition and long sentences. The narrator seems angry that he has had to work far harder than his rival as he describes his background in detail. For instance, a list of lowly jobs such as 'errand boy' and 'light porter' is used to emphasise how many steps it has taken for him to reach the top. The details are built up through long sentences with many additional clauses, which creates a fast rhythm for the reader. Together with the constant repetition of the pronoun 'I', this suggests that the narrator is so angry that he is actually shouting.

✓ Effective overview at start of answer.

✓ Clear point addresses the question and clear P-E-E structure is used to provide evidence and explanation.

✓ Good point that is fully developed with two pieces of evidence and an explanation that addresses the key focus of the question.

This answer is clearly focused on what the question asks. Always check that you do the same.

Now try this

Remember: it isn't enough just to identify a language or structural device. You also need to explain its effects. If you know it, use the technical name for a device, too.

Read lines 13–18 of the extract from *Samuel Lowgood's Revenge* by Mary E. Braddon on page 97.
Identify and comment on **two structural techniques** used in these lines about Christopher Weldon.
Use the improved sample answer above as a model.

Putting it into practice

In **Paper 2: Section A – Reading**, you'll need to respond to the **language** and **structure** in **non-fiction** texts. Read the extract from *Who'd Be a Paper Boy?* by John Crace on page 105. Then look at the exam-style question below and read the extracts from two students' answers.

Worked example

3 Analyse how the writer uses language and structure to interest and engage readers. Support your views with detailed reference to the text. **(15 marks)**

Turn to page 6 to revise skimming for the main idea

Writing about language and structure

For a question like this you should:

- ✓ spend about 15 minutes on your answer
- ✓ **read the whole text carefully** – this question is worth 15 marks and may not give you a specific focus to look out for
- ✓ identify the **main ideas**, then identify the **language** and **structural techniques** used
- ✓ refer to the **whole text** in your answer
- ✓ comment on the **language** and **structural techniques** used and their **effects**.

Sample answer extract

The writer starts with a list of three to emphasise the negative aspects of doing a paper round. This is followed by alliteration 'insult to injury' which creates humour as most readers will not feel that doing a paper round before school is very hard work.

After giving his opinion that in the past teenagers were happy to do this job, the writer then uses an expert opinion from a shop owner. The shop owner uses statistics, which makes her seem truthful.

✗ A clear point and identification of technique but no comment on effect.

✓ A clear point, identification of technique and explanation.

✗ Identification of techniques and clear reference to the extract, but no developed explanation of how this helps the writer's argument.

Improved sample answer

The writer uses a mixture of hyperbolic humorous opinions and statistics to argue that teenagers are too lazy to bother earning money. Starting with a list of three negative aspects of doing a paper round and then using the alliterative phrase 'insult to injury' creates humour as most readers will not feel that doing a paper round before school is hard work.

After giving his opinion that in the past teenagers were happy to do this job, the writer then provides expert evidence from a shop owner. The use of statistics from this expert, like '£20', provides concrete evidence that will persuade most adult readers that teenagers are lazy, as it seems like a lot of money for just 18 deliveries.

✓ Clear overview that identifies the main idea and argument used in the article.

✓ Clearly addresses both structure ('list of three') and language ('alliterative phrase') and uses the technical names for the techniques.

✓ Fully developed explanations.

Notice how this well-structured answer focuses on the 'how' in the question.

Now try this

Continue the 'Improved sample answer', aiming to identify at least **two** more points from the article.

Remember to look at sentence types when thinking about structure, and always look carefully at the beginning and end of the text to spot changes in tone.

Handling two texts

Paper 2: Section A – Reading there are two questions that ask you to refer to **both** of the **non-fiction texts** in your answer. The texts will always be linked by a **shared theme**, so will always have something in common. You will need to write about the **similarities** and **differences**. The questions on this page are sample questions and do not need to be answered.

Refer to both texts in your answer.

7 (a) The two texts are both about foreign travel. What similarities are there between the travel experiences of the two writers? Use evidence from both texts to support your answer. **(6 marks)**

Look at the marks available. This synthesis question is only worth 6 marks, so you need to take an overview and back this up with three or four points.

Question 7 (a)

The first of these two questions will ask you to **select information** from the **two non-fiction texts** and show your understanding by writing about them **together**. This is often called **synthesis**.

synthesise *verb*
To combine (a number of things) into a coherent whole.
Synonyms: combine, fuse, amalgamate, build a whole.

Turn to pages 35 and 36 to find out more about synthesising evidence

You will need to:

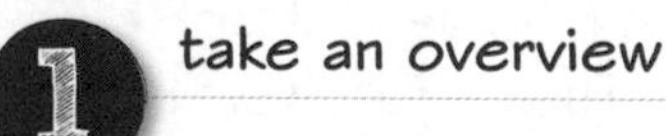

1. take an overview

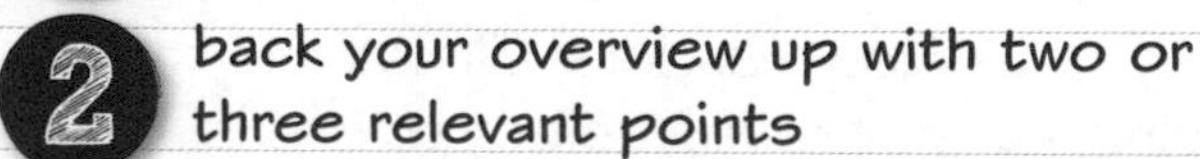

2. back your overview up with two or three relevant points
3. show a clear understanding of both texts.

Similarities and differences

The texts may be similar or different in various ways, for example in terms of:

- the ideas they express about the topic
- the perspective (point of view) they take about the topic
- the language they use
- the way they are structured.

Refer to both texts in your answer.

7 (b) Compare how the writers of Text 1 and Text 2 present their ideas and perspectives about foreign travel. Support your answer with detailed reference to the texts. **(14 marks)**

This question carries 14 marks, so spend some time revising how to compare effectively. You will need to compare the writer's ideas, as well as the actual language used.

Question 7 (b)

The second question will ask you to **compare** the two non-fiction texts.

compare *verb*
To examine (two or more objects, ideas, people, etc.) in order to note similarities and differences.

See pages 37–40 for more about comparing texts

You will need to:

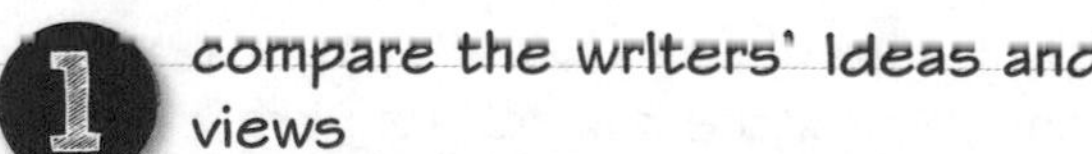

1. compare the writers' ideas and views
2. compare how the writers present these ideas and views through language and structure
3. give examples from the text and use them in a detailed comparison.

Now try this

1 Which of the two questions using both texts – 7 (a) and 7 (b) – should you spend the most time answering?
2 How many points do you need to make when answering the synthesis question, 7 (a)?
3 Which question requires you to look in detail at the language used in the texts?

Selecting evidence for synthesis

Question 7 (a) in **Paper 2: Section A – Reading** asks you to select information from **two non-fiction texts** and **write about both texts together**. This can be challenging and the first step is to **select evidence** that is relevant to the question.

Refer to both texts in your answer.

7 (a) The two texts are both about foreign travel. What similarities are there between the travel experiences of the two writers?
Use evidence from both texts to support your answer. **(6 marks)**

Highlight key words in the question to help you select relevant information and keep your answer focused.

To revise skim reading, see page 6

Selecting relevant information

For this type of question, you need to select **evidence that is relevant to the question**.

Skim read the longer text to find the main idea of each paragraph.

Aim to pick out **two pieces of evidence** that are relevant to the question.

Then **skim read** the second text.

Find **two pieces of evidence** that you can combine – or **synthesise** – with the evidence from the first text.

First text

Here are two pieces of evidence you might select from *The Hungry Cyclist*.

21st

Extracts from The Hungry Cyclist. *Full text on page 102. Lines 1–3.*

The air was cold and thin. Gasping for breath I said goodbye to a country I had fallen in love with and entered another.

Lines 5–7.

Gone were the smiles and friendly cheers of encouragement from the roadside. Gone were the picturesque colonial farmsteads with their flower-covered porches…

Point 1: The new country is harsh and the writer almost feels unwell when he arrives.

Point 2: The country is unwelcoming as nobody is smiling or friendly.

Skim reading the rest of the article shows that, unlike in *The Hungry Cyclist*, Bryson's experience of England does not improve. Therefore, the second part of the Bryson extract may not be relevant as you are less likely to find similarities.

Second text

Here are two pieces of evidence you might select from *Notes from a Small Island*.

Point 1: The weather is also bad, making the country seem immediately inhospitable.

Point 2: The country is unwelcoming as there are no people around and everywhere seems closed.

20th

Extracts from Notes from a Small Island. *Full text on page 103. Line 1.*

My first sight of England was on a foggy March night in 1973…

Lines 6–7.

… all the hotels and guesthouses appeared to be shut up for the night.

Now try this

Read the rest of the extracts from *The Hungry Cyclist* and *Notes from a Small Island* on pages 102 and 103. Find **one** further similarity that could be synthesised to answer exam-style question 7 (a) above.

Remember that there are only 6 marks available for this question. Skim read to maximise your time.

Synthesising evidence

Once you have selected the evidence you need to respond to **Question 7 (a)** in **Paper 2: Section A – Reading**, you need to **synthesise** the points in your answer.

Structuring your synthesis

To **synthesise the evidence** you have selected:

1. Start with an overview that sums up the main points of your answer.

   Make sure your overview includes key words from the question.

2. Use short quotations or briefly paraphrase your evidence.
3. Use **adverbials** to signpost the way through your synthesis.

Linking ideas

Use adverbials and linking phrases like these in your synthesis to show the similarities between the pieces of evidence:

- Similarly…
- Likewise…
- In the same way…
- Both writers feel…
- Both texts suggest…

The question is about *Notes from a Small Island* and *The Hungry Cyclist*, full texts on pages 103 and 102.

Look back at page 35 at the examples of information selected in answer to Paper 2 exam-style question 7 (a). Then look at how they are synthesised in an extract from a student's response in the Worked example.

Worked example

Refer to both texts in your answer.

7 (a) The two texts are both about foreign travel. What similarities are there between the travel experiences of the two writers? Use evidence from both texts to support your answer. **(6 marks)**

Both writers experience hardship when they first arrive in a new country. Both writers find the weather harsh: in Ecuador the air is 'cold and thin' and in England Bryson lands on a 'foggy March night'. Likewise, they do not feel welcomed, as in Ecuador the people do not smile when the writer cycles past and in England Bryson finds that all the hotels and guesthouses seem to be shut.

The overview uses key words from the question, which clearly signals that the answer will be relevant.

Clear signals that the answer is synthesising evidence from both texts.

Notice how short quotations have been used and how each sentence covers both texts. The final sentence paraphrases the extracts. This is a good way to answer if quotations would be too long.

Now try this

Write **one** more synthesis paragraph about *The Hungry Cyclist* and *Notes from a Small Island* on pages 103 and 102. You could use the point you selected on page 35 in your answer.

Remember to stick closely to the main focus of Question 7 (a) above.

Looking closely at language

Question 7 (b) in **Paper 2: Section A – Reading** will require you to look closely at both the **language** and the **structure** in **two non-fiction texts** and **compare** the **effects** that are created.

Analysing the texts

Before you can answer the comparison question you need to look **very** closely at the texts and explore the **language** and **structure** the writer has chosen to use. You could ask yourself:

Remember that you must not write about one text without making a comparative point about the other.

What literary or rhetorical devices has the writer chosen to use? What effects do they have?

What types and lengths of sentences has the writer used? What effect do they have?

To revise rhetorical devices, turn to pages 25 and 26

Turn to pages 28 and 29 for a reminder about sentence structure

The use of a list and pattern of three emphasise how inadequate and nervous he was on his first day.

The short single-clause sentence contrasts with the long multi-clause sentences that deliver the anecdote in the opening paragraph and changes the tone of the article to one that is more serious.

21st

Extract from The History of London's Black Cabs. *Full text on page 104. Lines 1–8.*

When I picked up my first fare in Covent Garden last month, I couldn't even open the passenger doors. I had two gentlemen fresh from dinner in Langley Street, and I was panicking, pressing all the buttons I could find, fumbling with keys. Nonetheless they were delighted when I told them they were my first, and that consequently the ride – as goes the cabbie tradition – was free, to wherever they wanted to go. Clapham Junction, as it happened, though they might as well have said Tuxedo Junction as far as my frayed nerves were concerned.

When I started learning the Knowledge of London in October 2008, the examiner told us it was the hardest thing we would ever do. He wasn't exaggerating.

Build-up of negative verbs with connotations of nervous struggle; 'frayed' suggests he is falling apart under the pressure.

Opens with an anecdote to elicit the reader's empathy and establish the writer's knowledge about the topic.

What connotations are created by the language the writer has chosen? What tone does the language create?

What structure has the writer used? How do the opening and conclusion of the text differ? What effect does this have?

Now try this

Turn to pages 14 and 15 to refresh your quotation and P-E-E skills

Read the second paragraph (lines 7–17) of *The History of London's Black Cabs* by Ian Beetlestone on page 104. Identify **two** further points you could make about language and/or structure. Write a P-E-E paragraph about each point, supporting your points with evidence from the text and commenting on its effect.

Remember, for a full answer to a question like this you need to compare two texts and consider ideas and perspectives.

Had a look ☐ Nearly there ☐ Nailed it! ☐

Planning to compare

In **Paper 2: Section A – Reading**, the comparison question – **Question 7 (b)** – is the most challenging. In this question, you will be asked to **compare two non-fiction texts**. You will write a better answer if you set aside a couple of minutes to **plan** before you start. Look at the Paper 2 exam-style question below, then at one student's planning.

Refer to both texts in your answer.

7 (b) Compare how the writers of *Notes from a Grandmother* and *Who'd Be a Paper Boy?* present their ideas and perspectives about teenagers.
Support your answer with detailed reference to the texts. **(14 marks)**

Approaches to comparing

When comparing two texts you could:

- identify similar language or structural techniques in both texts and then explain the effects they create OR
- find similar effects (such as tone or ideas) and explain the different techniques the writers have used to achieve these effects.

Extract from Who'd Be a Paper Boy? *Full text on page 105. Lines 1–18.*

It's cold, it's dark and you've got to bolt your breakfast before dragging a bag full of papers round the streets. To add insult to injury, you then have to go to school. So who would be bothered with a paper round? Almost no one these days, it seems.

Twenty years ago, a paper round was one of the few ways for a teenager to earn a few quid to squander on a packet of No 6 and a bottle of cider, and the kids who did it generally took it seriously.

- Pattern of three and hyperbole to exaggerate negative side of paper rounds.
- Alliteration for humour.
- Rhetorical question to involve audience.
- Colloquial language for emphasis.

Extract from Notes from a Grandmother. *Full text on page 101. Lines 1–5.*

There is life after teenage. Hard to believe when you're facing a screaming virago or sullen, resentful stranger. You are now a fallen idol. From Mum! who could put everything right, you have become Mum! who understands nothing.

Before you throw in the towel, or leap from the bedroom window, or throw your offspring out of the door, find a quiet moment. And consider.

- Emotive adjectives used at start to exaggerate negative behaviour of teenagers.
- Suggests mothers lose their power over teenagers; they become difficult to manage.
- Pattern of three and hyperbole to exaggerate negative effect of teenage behaviour on mothers.
- Short sentence to suggest change in tone.

Now try this

Read *Who'd Be a Paper Boy?* on page 105 and *Notes from a Grandmother* on page 101.
Using the student's planning notes about language above, write a paragraph in answer to Question 7 (b). Use P-E-E to structure your paragraph and remember to refer to both texts.

Remember to signal your comparison:

- similarities: similarly, both, likewise, in the same way
- differences: however, on the other hand, whereas, unlike

Comparing ideas and perspectives

When **comparing** texts in **Paper 2** you will also need to write about the writers' **ideas and perspectives**. You will need to **skim read** (see page 6) to identify the main ideas and perspectives in each text. You will also need to use your **language comparison skills** (see pages 37 and 38). The texts in **Paper 2** will be linked by **theme**.

Refer to both texts in your answer.

7 (b) Compare how the writers of *Notes from a Grandmother* and *Who'd be a Paper Boy?* present their ideas and perspectives about teenagers.

Support your answer with detailed reference to the texts. **(14 marks)**

You need to use quotations in your answer.

Each time you make a point about the first text, find a similarity/difference in the second text. This will help you write an equal amount about both texts.

Comparing ideas and identifying perspectives

1. Start with the longer text and skim read it to find the main idea of each paragraph.
2. Use your 'planning to compare' skills to find language and structure points you can use to explain how the main ideas are presented.
3. Identify the perspective of the writer – how does he/she feel about the theme?
4. Then do the same for the shorter text.

Difference in language and effect: Crace's hyperbole has a sarcastic tone, suggesting 'kids' do not actually want to 'get out of bed' and work. In contrast, *Notes from a Grandmother* uses repetition of 'they' to suggest that teenagers have serious concerns.

Similarity in main idea: both texts deal with teenagers' problems.

Difference in perspective: Crace's sarcastic tone and use of the colloquial 'bottom line' suggests he has no sympathy for modern teenagers as they are lazy. In contrast, the perspective in *Notes from a Grandmother* is that teenagers deserve sympathy and respect as they 'do think' and are concerned about important issues.

21st

Extract from Who'd Be a Paper Boy? *Full text on page 105. Line 5–19.*

You can have some sympathy for the kids. Standards in literacy and numeracy have fallen so steeply that it can be a real struggle identifying door names and numbers, and the Sunday papers are now so heavy that your averagely obese teenager just doesn't have the strength or stamina for the job. But the bottom line is that most kids can no longer be bothered to get out of bed for £20.

20th

Extract from Notes from a Grandmother. *Full text on page 101. Lines 9–12.*

Our teenagers are troubled. They are uncertain. They are emotionally insecure. They are worried about future unemployment, by the continued demolition of their world, by pollution, by the threat of nuclear war. Our teenagers do think, and where rational thought fails to provide solutions, they *feel*.

Now try this

Read the last two paragraphs of *Who'd Be a Paper Boy?* and *Notes from a Grandmother* on pages 105 and 101. Write a paragraph comparing the final ideas and perspectives presented by the writers.

Had a look ☐ Nearly there ☐ Nailed it! ☐

Answering a comparison question

One challenge in answering the **comparison question** on **Paper 2** is showing your understanding fully. To do this, you need to use an effective structure for your answer.

Structure

Aim to make direct comparisons.

You could **focus on one language feature** or its effect in the first text, then compare it to a similar feature or effect in the second text.

You could also **explore differences** – for example, writing about the different tones of the two texts and how language is used to achieve them.

Linking words and phrases

Use adverbials to signpost the way through your answer.

For example, you could **signpost a similarity** using adverbials like: 'Similarly…' or 'In the same way…'

To **signpost a difference** you can use adverbials like: 'However…' or 'On the other hand…'

Worked example

Write a brief overview in one sentence summarising the two texts and their purposes.

Both texts are about… but **Text 1** aims to… while **Text 2** tries to…

Write about a language or structural feature in **Text 1**, supported with evidence and an explanation of its effect on the reader.

Text 1 uses…

Similarly, **Text 2** uses…

Use an adverbial to link a point about a similar language or structural feature in **Text 2**. Support this with evidence and explanation.

Both texts use emotive language. For example, **Text 1**…

This makes the reader realise that…

On the other hand, **Text 2** uses emotive language to achieve a different effect…

The writer has created a humorous tone in **Text 1**. He has done this by using puns such as…

However, the writer of **Text 2** has created a much more disturbing tone by…

Getting it right

Remember:

- you can write about a difference – for example, a similar language feature that has a different effect in the two texts, or how the writers have used language to support their different purposes, appealed to different audiences or created different ideas and perspectives
- you should always make it clear which text you are referring to – for example, using the writer's name (e.g. 'Crace suggests …'), the form of the text (e.g. 'The speech shows …'), the name or title of the text (e.g. 'In *Notes from a Grandmother*…'), or the number of the text (e.g. 'Text 1 suggests …').

Now try this

Read the texts *Who'd Be a Paper Boy?* on page 105 and *Notes from a Grandmother* on page 101. Use the structure in the worked example to write the **first paragraph** of an answer to Question 7 (b) on page 39.

Try to use the words 'idea' and 'perspective' in your answer. Remember to spend a couple of minutes planning before you start to write.

Putting it into practice

In **Paper 2: Section A – Reading** you will need to **compare** the writers' **ideas and perspectives**, and how they are presented, in **two non-fiction texts**. Read the extracts from *The Hungry Cyclist* and *Notes from a Small Island* on pages 102 and 103. Then look at the exam-style question below and read the extracts from two students' answers.

Worked example

Refer to both texts in your answer.

7 (b) Compare how the writers of *The Hungry Cyclist* and *Notes from a Small Island* present their ideas and perspectives about the places they visit.
Support your answer with detailed reference to the texts. **(14 marks)**

Comparing writers' ideas and perspectives

For a question like this you should:

- ✓ spend about 14 minutes on your answer
- ✓ highlight the **key words** in the **question**
- ✓ spend a couple of minutes **planning** your answer before you start writing
- ✓ look at the **whole** of **both texts** to find points relevant to the question
- ✓ identify the **language** and **structural techniques** used and comment on how they help the writer to get across their **ideas, perspectives** and **arguments**.

Sample answer extract

Kevill-Davies's article is about travelling to Ecuador and Bryson's book is about his experiences in England. Kevill-Davies does not like Ecuador at the start as it is 'cold' and he uses a list of three negative types of people, including 'pickpockets', to show how unwelcome he feels. Bryson starts with negative feelings about the weather but seems to enjoy England as he says he feels like 'Bulldog Drummond', which has connotations of being an adventure hero.

✗ Some comments about the main idea, but no overview or comparison given.

✓ Examples of language and structural ('at the start') techniques, with some explanation of their effect.

✗ Examples of language and structural technique with some explanation, but no comparison.

Improved sample answer

Both writers encounter poor weather when they arrive in unfamiliar countries, but whereas Kevill-Davies's perspective is very negative when he first arrives, Bryson begins his travels with a positive point of view despite the weather. Kevill-Davies begins his description of Ecuador negatively with a short sentence summing up the weather as 'cold and thin'. He then follows this with a list of three negative types of people, including 'pickpockets', to show how unwelcoming the country is. Bryson also starts with a description of the weather as 'foggy' but unlike Kevill-Davies he finds the silence exciting as he feels like 'Bulldog Drummond', which has connotations of an adventure hero.

✓ Clear overview comparing the initial ideas and perspectives of the writers.

✓ Fully developed point about the language techniques used in one text.

✓ Similarities/differences between the texts are clearly signalled.

✓ Fully developed explanation of effects.

Now try this

Complete the 'Improved sample answer' with **at least one** more paragraph. Try to pick up on both similarities and differences in the language and structure.

Remember to use evidence from **both** texts to show **how** the writers present their ideas.

Had a look ☐ Nearly there ☐ Nailed it! ☐

Evaluating a text

Both papers will have a question that tests your ability to **evaluate** texts. The questions on this page are sample questions and do not need to be answered.

Approaching evaluation

A useful way to think about evaluation is to look at **how well** something is achieved, rather than simply how it is achieved. For example, if you are asked about how successfully a writer creates tension, you do not need to look in detail at the connotations of individual words and techniques. Instead, you need to look at the **text as a whole**, and **discuss how well** the writer has created tension **overall**.

evaluate *(verb)* To assess something and form an idea about its value. *Synonyms:* form an opinion of, make up one's mind about, analyse

Approaching an evaluation question

1. Read the question – This will tell you what specific aspect of the text to evaluate
2. Read the text – Identify any key ideas, events, themes and settings that relate to the question
3. Annotate key quotations – Look at the **ideas, events, themes** and **settings.** How and why are they used to create effects?
   - **Ideas:** what does the writer think or believe? **Events:** what happens or is described?
   - **Themes:** what is the text's tone or purpose? **Settings:** where and when do things occur?
4. Plan your answer – Use inference to explain and evaluate the effects
5. Write your answer – Make a judgement – **how well** has the focus been achieved? Explain your ideas in detail and support them with evidence

This Paper 1 exam-style question is about *Little Dorrit*, full text on page 96.

4 In this extract, there is an attempt to create a sense of danger about the prison.
Evaluate how successfully this is achieved.
Support your views with detailed reference to the text.
(15 marks)

This Paper 2 exam-style question is about *Notes from a Small Island*, full text on page 103.

6 Bill Bryson attempts to engage the reader through the description of the problems he faces on his first night in England.
Evaluate how successfully this is achieved.
Support your views with detailed reference to the text.
(15 marks)

Look carefully at the focus of the question:

- For Paper 1 you need to look at an **effect** that is created – make sure you look for this effect throughout the **whole** text.
- For Paper 2 you need to look at **one specific aspect of the extract** – in this example, you'd need to focus on descriptions of the problems faced, rather than analysing everything that happens.

Both questions tell you to use 'detailed reference to the text'. You can use quotations or paraphrase the text to do this.

Go to page 14 for a reminder about using evidence

Now try this

Look at Paper 2 exam-style question 6 above. Follow steps 1 to 3 in the flow diagram on this page to annotate key quotations in the extract from *Notes from a Small Island* by Bill Bryson on page 103. Think carefully about which quotations would help you to answer the question. As this is a non-fiction text, it is a good idea to start by identifying the writer's key ideas and themes.

Evaluating a text: fiction

In **Paper 1** you will need to evaluate a **fiction** text.

This Paper 1 exam-style question is about *The Half-Brothers*.

4 In this extract, there is an attempt to create a sense of danger.
Evaluate how successfully this is achieved.
Support your views with detailed reference to the text. **(15 marks)**

This **Paper 1** evaluation question is worth **15 marks.** You will be asked to refer to **one specific effect** in the text. Here, this is 'a sense of danger'.

Getting it right

When answering an evaluation question:

- **DO** quote or paraphrase to back up your points
- **DON'T** analyse language or structure in detail – for example, you could observe 'The phrase "wild boggy moor" foreshadows the danger to come', but you don't need to discuss the connotations of the words or the phrase itself
- **REMEMBER** that paraphrasing can be particularly useful when you don't need to give a detailed analysis.

19th

Extract from The Half-Brothers. *Full text on page 99. Lines 3–9.*

The right path was clear enough in the day-time, although at several points two or three exactly similar diverged from the same place; but when there was a good light, the traveller was guided by the sight of distant objects,—a piece of rock,—a fall in the ground—which were quite invisible to me now. I plucked up a brave heart, however, and took what seemed to me the right road. It was wrong, nevertheless, and led me whither I knew not, but to some wild boggy moor where the solitude seemed painful, intense, as if never footfall of man had come thither to break the silence.

Settings – Setting is important from the start of the extract with the build-up of close descriptions, for instance of the paths. This establishes the setting, and the fact that it is dark, as an important part of the story. As it is a 'wild boggy moor', this creates a feeling of impending danger.

Events – The narrator takes the wrong turning and becomes lost early in the extract. This foreshadows the danger to come, especially when combined with the sense of danger created in the description of the setting.

Settings and events are usually most relevant in a fiction text, but you could also look at the ideas and themes. For instance, in *The Half-Brothers* there is the supernatural (an idea) and fear (a theme). How do they contribute to the sense of danger?

Note how this student:

- uses a mixture of paraphrase (for example, 'takes the wrong turning ...') and quotation (for example, 'wild boggy moor') as evidence
- addresses both **how** and **why** the settings/events are used.

Now try this

Read the whole of the extract from *The Half-Brothers* by Elizabeth Gaskell on page 99. Identify **two** more ways in which the setting and/or the events are used to create a sense of danger.

Had a look ☐ Nearly there ☐ Nailed it! ☐

Evaluating a text: non-fiction

In **Paper 2** you will need to evaluate a **non-fiction** text.

This Paper 2 exam-style question is about *Notes from a Grandmother*. Full text on page 101.

6 The writer attempts to engage the reader through the description of life with teenagers. Evaluate how successfully this is achieved. Support your views with detailed reference to the text. **(15 marks)**

This **Paper 2** evaluation question is worth **15 marks.** You will be asked to look at **one specific aspect** of the text. Here, this is 'the description of life with teenagers'.

Getting it right

When you are evaluating:

- use the **key words** in the **question** to keep your answer focused
- **skim read**, then read the text in more **detail**
- look at the **ideas** and **themes**, forming your **opinion** and **identifying evidence**
- use your **inference** skills to **explain** and **assess** the text.

Ideas and themes are likely to be the most relevant areas to look at in a non-fiction text. However, for some non-fiction texts it may also be useful to look at events and settings.

Extract from Notes from a Grandmother. *Full text on page 101. Lines 1–8.*

There is life after teenage. Hard to believe when you're facing a screaming virago or sullen, resentful stranger. You are now a fallen idol. From Mum! who could put everything right, you have become Mum! who understands nothing.

Before you throw in the towel, or leap from the bedroom window, or throw your offspring out of the door, find a quiet moment. And consider.

Your child has stepped into a world beyond your reach. The rules, customs, clothes and hairstyles are not within the scope of your experience. Pressures and temptations increase with each decade.

Ideas – The main idea is the behaviour of teenagers. From the start, the text suggests they are difficult to live with and no longer prepared to listen to parents who 'understand nothing'.

Themes – Readers are encouraged to 'find a quiet moment' to 'consider' and this suggests that advice will be a theme throughout the text. This will also encourage readers and reassure them that life with teenagers can get better.

Events – The writer describes events in a teenager's life, as they become a different species with strange 'rules, customs, clothes and hairstyles'. This is engaging as readers will feel the writer really understands their experiences as parents.

An evaluative sentence that explains why the text is engaging.

A clear evaluation of effect.

When evaluating:

- keep the focus of the question in mind as you read the text – this part of the text is relevant as it describes how and why teenagers are difficult to live with
- look at the structure of the text – for example, this opening appears to offer advice, so check the middle and end to see if the tone or theme is the same.

Identify the main idea in the text you are evaluating. Themes are similar to ideas. You could think of themes as the tone or purpose of the text.

Now try this

Read the rest of the extract from *Notes from a Grandmother* on page 101. Identify **two** more points you could make to answer evaluation question 6 above.

Remember to look at ideas, themes and – for this text – events.

Turn to page 30 to revise structure in non-fiction

Putting it into practice

In **Paper 1: Section A – Reading**, you'll need to **evaluate** a **fiction** text and **support** and **explain** your evaluation with **evidence** from the text. Read the extract from *The Adventures of Tom Sawyer* by Mark Twain on page 98. Then look at the exam-style question below and read the extracts from two students' answers.

Worked example

4 In this extract, there is an attempt to show the different reactions the children have to the danger they face.
Evaluate how successfully this is achieved.
Support your views with detailed reference to the text. **(15 marks)**

Evaluating non-fiction

For a question like this you should:

- ✓ spend about 30 minutes on your answer
- ✓ read the question carefully and **highlight the main focus**
- ✓ refer to the **whole text**
- ✓ look at how **ideas, events, themes** and **settings** are used to create **effects**
- ✓ use inference and evidence from the text to explain your ideas and assess the effect of the text.

Sample answer extract

Tom is shown to be calm and sensible when he tells Becky that they need to stay near the water. He is also thoughtful as he remains 'silent a moment' before comforting Becky and giving her positive answers when she worries about whether they have been missed.

✓ Clear point, looking at events and showing clear focus on the question.

✓ Use of quotation as evidence.

✗ Retells the story rather than evaluating the text.

Avoid referring to characters as if they are real people. Instead, use sentence starters like 'The writer uses ...', 'The writer suggests ...' or 'The character is presented as ...'.

Improved sample answer

Throughout the extract Tom is presented as calm and sensible in the face of danger. This contrasts with Becky, who reacts with tears and fright. Dialogue is used to emphasise the different reactions. Whilst Becky is shown attempting to be cheerful about the cake, she 'dropped the sentence', which suggests she is too frightened to talk about what faces them. A long exchange of dialogue about whether they will be found shows Tom to be calm and reassuring. This is effective as it contrasts with Becky's worried comments like 'When would they miss us, Tom?'

✓ Clear overview at the start of the answer that uses key words from the question.

✓ Good use of evidence with explanation that addresses the focus of the question.

✓ Clear paraphrasing refers to the text without the use of lengthy quotations.

✓ The phrase 'This is effective' indicates a clear evaluation.

Note the use of the evaluative phrase 'This is effective ...'. Use phrases like this to show you are making judgements about how successful the text is.

Now try this

Complete the 'Improved sample answer' with **one** further evaluative point.

The sample answers above look at **events** (what happens) and consider how the children react to their **setting**. You could also think about the main **idea** of being trapped, or being a hero.

Had a look ☐ Nearly there ☐ Nailed it! ☐

Putting it into practice

In **Paper 2: Section A – Reading**, you'll need to **evaluate** a **non-fiction** text and **support** and **explain** your evaluation with **evidence** from the text. Read the extract from *Angela's Ashes* by Frank McCourt on page 100. Then look at the exam-style question below and read the extracts from two students' answers.

Worked example

6 Frank McCourt attempts to engage the reader by presenting himself as unprepared for his first day at work.
Evaluate how successfully this is achieved.
Support your views with detailed reference to the text. **(15 marks)**

Evaluating fiction

For a question like this you should:

- ✓ spend about 15 minutes on your answer
- ✓ read the question carefully and **highlight the main focus**
- ✓ refer to the **whole text**
- ✓ look at how **ideas, events, themes** and **settings** are used to create **effects**
- ✓ use **inference** and **evidence from the text** to **explain** your ideas and assess the **effect** of the text.

Sample answer extract

Frank McCourt does not understand the joke about the lavatories and this shows him to be too young to start work. Also he has brought a note from his mother. The woman in the telegram office is unsympathetic and 'cackles' when mocking Frank. This engages the reader as it creates sympathy for him.

✓ Clear evidence and some explanation.

✗ Clear evidence but lacks explanation.

✗ Clear evidence and an evaluation but does not address the focus of the question.

Make sure your evaluation is focused on the key words in the question.

Improved sample answer

The main idea of the extract is starting work, and Frank is shown to be unprepared from the beginning of the extract as he does not understand the joke about the lavatories. This establishes as a theme his naivety, or immaturity, which is continued throughout the extract. For instance, an immature tone is evident as he has brought a note from his mother, has obviously not realised that it is necessary to wash before his first day at work and needs his aunt to help him buy clothes. This is engaging as it creates sympathy for Frank: readers will be on his side and want him to succeed in the job.

✓ Good overview that shows a clear focus on the question and considers the main ideas and themes.

✓ Relevant evidence from the opening and slightly later in the text shows understanding of the whole extract.

✓ Clear evaluation of effects.

In Paper 2, the non-fiction text you evaluate may be from the 20th century. Remember that some older texts can express ideas and views that differ from those held by most people today. Be careful not to dismiss them simply as 'old-fashioned'.

Now try this

Continue the 'Improved sample answer' above by writing **one** further paragraph.

Writing questions: an overview

Both papers of the English Language GCSE include a **Writing** section (Section B). There are different types of writing task in each paper.

For a reminder about how the English Language GCSE is structured, turn to page 1

Paper 1: Section B – Writing

Imaginative writing → Write **one** response **from a choice of two** tasks

Paper 1 tests your ability to write **imaginatively**.

Paper 2: Section B – Writing

Transactional writing → Answer **one question from a choice of two.**

Paper 2 tests your ability to write for **different audiences and purposes**.

Find out more about the Paper 1 and Paper 2 reading texts on page 2

It is possible that both writing questions in Paper 2 will ask you to write in the same form, for example, a letter. If this happens, then the audience and/or purpose of the tasks will be different.

On **both papers**, look out for a note like this:
Your response will be marked for the accurate and appropriate use of vocabulary, spelling, punctuation and grammar.
You need to:

- vary the length and types of sentence you use
- spell and punctuate correctly
- use interesting and effective words.

Make sure you leave time to proofread your work when you've finished writing!

Assessment objectives

Assessment objectives are the **skills** you are tested on in the exam questions. For Writing, the assessment objectives are the same for both papers.

Remember what skills you will be tested on for each component. The exam papers will not remind you.

Assessment objective 5 tests your ability to:

- communicate clearly, effectively, and imaginatively, selecting and adapting tone, style and register for different forms, purposes and audiences

Select the right form for your writing and use the most appropriate language for your audience.

- organise information and ideas, using structural and grammatical features to support coherence and cohesion of texts.

Use sentences and paragraphs to organise and structure your writing so the meaning is clear.

Assessment objective 6 tests your ability to use a range of vocabulary and sentence structures for clarity, purpose and effect, with accurate spelling and punctuation.

Now try this

Answer the following questions using the information on this page.

1 The questions in one paper require you to use language that is appropriate for a specific audience. Which paper is this?
2 How many writing questions do you need to answer for each paper?
3 Which paper or papers will require you to vary the length and type of your sentences?

Writing questions: Paper 1

Paper 1: Section B – Writing will test the quality of your **imaginative writing** skills. The questions on this page are sample questions and do not need to be answered.

Planning your time

It is important to plan and use your time in the exam carefully. Every minute counts!

Total time for Paper 1 – 1 hour and 45 minutes

You should spend about **45 minutes** on **Section B – Writing**. For example:

- 10 minutes planning
- 35 minutes writing.

You could choose to spend just 30 minutes writing, leaving you five minutes to check and proofread your answer.

Planning your answer

It is worth spending some time **planning** your writing before you start. The more you plan, the less time you will waste when you are actually writing.

Planning for imaginative writing is covered in more detail on page 61

Understanding the questions

These are examples of the two types of questions you will find in the exam.

In the exam, make sure you read the questions carefully.

5 Write about a time when you, or someone you know, was tempted into taking revenge.
Your response could be real or imagined.
(40 marks)

6 Look at the images A and B on page 106.
Write about a deserted house.
Your response could be real or imagined.
You may wish to base your response on one of the images. **(40 marks)**

The questions will not tell you which form your writing should take, but you should write in prose.

The word 'may' tells you that you do not *have* to use the images, but you *must* still focus on the theme of the question. Here, this is 'a deserted house'.

Find out more about prose on page 60

How the marks work

In **Paper 1: Section B – Writing**, there are **40 marks** available:

Assessment objective 5 (communication and organisation)	24 marks
Assessment objective 6 (spelling, punctuation, grammar and vocabulary)	16 marks

See page 47 for more detail on the assessment objectives for writing

Now try this

Choose one of the exam-style questions above. Write the title as a heading and then spend five minutes jotting down as many ideas as you can, in the form of a spider diagram, for example.

Remember: in the exam you will need to spend a further five minutes organising your ideas into an effective structure. Find out more on page 62.

Writing questions: Paper 2

Paper 2: Section B – Writing will test the quality of your **transactional writing** skills. You need to show you can write effectively for **different audiences and purposes**. The questions on this page are sample questions and do not need to be answered.

Planning your time

Remember use your time in the exam carefully.

Total time for Paper 2 – 2 hours

You should spend about **45 minutes** on **Section B – Writing**. For example:

- 10 minutes planning
- 35 minutes writing.

You could choose to spend just 30 minutes writing, leaving you five minutes to check and proofread your answer.

See page 47 for more detail on the assessment objectives for writing

What is transactional writing?

This type of writing is usually formal and includes letters, articles or reports, as well as reviews, speeches, and even information guides, autobiographies, travel writing and obituaries.

transactional writing *noun*
Writing to get things done, to inform or persuade a particular audience to understand or do something

How the marks work

In **Paper 2: Section B – Writing**, there are **40 marks** available:

Assessment objective 5 (communication and organisation)	24 marks
Assessment objective 6 (spelling, punctuation, grammar and vocabulary)	16 marks

Understanding the questions

These are examples of the two types of questions you will find in the exam.

Form – This clearly tells you what form your writing must take. Here, it is a letter.

Audience – The purpose suggests an adult audience that you do not know, so a formal style will be most appropriate.

Purpose – Clues will be given in the question. Here, the task is a letter of application, which suggests that you will need to **write persuasively** in order to present yourself as the best candidate for the job.

8 Write a letter to your local radio station applying for a part-time position as the presenter of their new show for students.

In your letter you could:

- state why you are interested in the position
- describe the experience and skills that make you a good candidate
- explain how you would help them to increase their number of listeners

… as well as including any other ideas you may have. **(40 marks)**

9 Write an article for a newspaper exploring the benefits of taking a gap year before university.

You could write about:

- the activities people choose for gap years and the countries they choose to visit, e.g. volunteering, travelling, Africa
- the advantages for a teenager of taking a gap year before university
- what should be considered before taking a gap year

… as well as any other ideas you may have. **(40 marks)**

Now try this

Look at Question 9. Don't try to answer it. Instead, make notes about:

- the form your writing should take
- the purpose of the writing
- the audience you should write for.

Writing for a purpose: imaginative

The focus of **Paper 1: Section B – Writing** is **imaginative writing**. There are several techniques you can use to develop your ideas and engage the reader.

The five senses

I could feel the steady trickle of sweat across my forehead and down my temples, and as I stumbled over the cracked earth I was pursued by the furious buzzing of flies.

Use of the senses of touch ('feel') and sound ('buzzing') makes the description **vivid** and **engages** the reader.

When you describe a place or an experience, help the reader to imagine they are there – use the five senses of sight, sound, touch, taste and smell.

Many students only write about what can be seen. Use the other senses to help your writing stand out.

Figurative language

Used carefully and imaginatively, **figurative language**, or **imagery**, can create powerful pictures in the reader's mind. Figurative devices include:

- similes
- metaphors
- personification.

Use your imagination! Similes like 'cool as a cucumber' and 'flat as a pancake' are not very original or creative.

Narrative voice and feelings

Unless the exam paper tells you which narrative voice to use, you can choose to write in the first or third person. Remember:

- a **first person narration** can give the reader **a sense of closeness to the narrator**
- You must stick to the narrative voice you choose throughout your answer!

Turn to pages 23 and 79 for a reminder about narrative voice in fiction

Describing the narrator's feelings can bring descriptive writing to life, too:

✗ I smiled and felt very relaxed.

The reader is told the narrator feels relaxed but is not drawn into the scene.

✓ A smile spread slowly across my lips and I felt all the tension drain from my limbs as I leant back into the chair and closed my eyes.

The verbs help the reader imagine the narrator's physical relaxation.

Language choice

The **quality** of your description is more important than the **quantity** of words you use. It is more effective to use fewer, well-chosen words. For example:

This student answer creates a much more immediate image than the long sentence in the student answer below.

I danced across the road.

I walked cheerfully with a spring in my step across the road like I was dancing.

Avoid overloading your writing with figurative devices or descriptive techniques.

Now try this

Write the **first paragraph** of your response to this **Paper 1** exam-style question.

5 Write about a time when you were desperately looking forward to an event.
Your response could be real or imagined. **(40 marks)**

Try to use:

- at least two different senses
- verbs to show, rather than tell, how you felt
- at least one example of figurative language.

Writing for a purpose: inform, explain, review

For **Paper 2: Section B – Writing** you will need to show you can write effectively for **different transactional purposes.** Transactional writing includes texts that **inform, explain** or **review.**

Also see pages 56–58 for more about form

Features to inform, explain and review

Headings and sub-headings

- especially useful for **information texts**
- use **headings** to organise the text
- use relevant **sub-headings** to make information easy to find.

Facts and statistics

These suggest the information you are giving can be trusted.

If you are writing about the same topic as the reading texts in Section A, you could use facts and statistics from either or both of them. If not, you can make them up to suit the point you are making.

Be careful: the facts and statistics need to be believable!

Structure

Information and explanation texts:

- are usually **organised chronologically**
- have **time** or **temporal adverbials** which provide signposts:

First... Then... Next... Finally...

Reviews:

- usually start with a brief **summary**
- include the reviewer's **opinions**
- **avoid lengthy descriptions** of events.

Tone

Tone means the mood of a text, for example, serious, instructive, casual.

- Use a **formal tone** to suggest to the reader that the information is reliable.
- Use **Standard English.**

Depending on your audience and topic, you could use humour – but take care not to overdo it!

Language

Texts that inform, explain or review are factual, so avoid using too much figurative language.

See page 20 for more about figurative devices

Getting it right

You can still use figurative language like similes and metaphors, but make sure the techniques you use support the purpose of the text. For example, if you are informing, explaining or reviewing, make sure you don't start describing!

Now try this

Look at this **Paper 2** exam-style question and then complete the tasks below:

1 List five subheadings you could use to organise your writing.

2 Write a sentence describing the tone you would use in this task.

3 Write down any facts or statistics you could include in your writing, for example, the typical number of students in a class.

9 Write a guide for your school newspaper about how to survive your first year at secondary school.

You could write about:

- what secondary school is like, for example, the uniform, the behaviour policy
- what subjects are available and what they are like
- the sports and extra-curricular activities.

(40 marks)

Had a look ☐ Nearly there ☐ Nailed it! ☐

Writing for a purpose: argue and persuade

Transactional writing also includes texts that **argue** or **persuade**.

Find out more about form on pages 56–58

Key points

The power of your argument or persuasion relies on the strength of your key points.

To argue:

> There are those who claim that modern teenagers are lazy and uncaring, yet nothing could be further from the truth. In fact, the numbers of teenagers actively involved in charitable causes is on the rise…

Choose points which highlight:

- why you are right
- why those who disagree are wrong.

To persuade:

> With the rise and rise of social media, it is hardly surprising that many teenagers today are comfortably cocooned in their own online oasis. What better way to coax them out into the daylight than to get them working with local charities…

Choose points which highlight:

- what is wrong with the way things are
- how your ideas will make things better.

Rhetorical devices

To engage your reader and add power to your argument or persuasive writing, use:

- rhetorical questions
- direct address
- repetition
- lists
- alliteration
- contrast
- pattern of three
- emotive language
- hyperbole.

Evidence

Always support **each** of your key points with convincing evidence. For example:

- facts or statistics
- an expert opinion
- an example from your own experience.

Linking ideas

Use adverbials to signpost the path your argument is going to follow.

To build your argument:

- furthermore…
- additionally/in addition…
- moreover…

To introduce counter-arguments:

- however…
- yet…
- on the other hand…

Also see page 71 for more about adverbials

To explain and develop your points:

- consequently/as a consequence…
- therefore…

Counter-arguments

Think about how your readers might disagree with you, and then point out why they are wrong. This is called a making a 'counter-argument' and is an effective way of dealing with opposing ideas. For example:

> Some people think that teenagers are lazy and uncaring. However, it is the media who give us these negative images...

Use adverbials to show that you are rejecting an opposing view.

Now try this

Look at this **Paper 2** exam-style question and then complete the tasks.

1 Note down three key points you could use in your answer.

2 Make a counter-argument.

3 Write three sentences using two different rhetorical devices.

8 Write a letter to your local MP giving your views about animal experimentation.

In your letter you could:

- describe the ways animals are used in experiments
- state the benefits of experimenting on animals, for example, medical advances
- explain the disadvantages of experimenting on animals. **(40 marks)**

Writing for an audience

For **Paper 2: Section B – Writing** you will need to show you can write effectively for **different audiences.**

Identifying the audience

In some questions, the audience (person or people) you are writing for may be clearly **stated**:

> **8** Write a letter to your local MP giving …
> **(40 marks)**

Your writing **must address** an adult (the MP) and will require a formal response. As you are writing to a specific person, you could engage them directly by referring to their role – for example 'As a Member of Parliament, you should …'.

Other questions may only **imply** (hint at) an audience:

> **9** Write an article for your local newspaper …
> **(40 marks)**

For this type of question you will need to think carefully about **who** would read this type of newspaper. In this case, it will probably be adults but may include teenagers.

Writing for an adult audience

When writing for an adult audience, you will usually need to write in a formal style and use Standard English.

You should avoid non-standard English:

- texting language (e.g. LOL)
- slang (e.g. I was gutted)
- double negatives (e.g. I ain't never done that).

Worked example

> **8** Write an information guide for parents about helping their children with homework …
> **(40 marks)**

Parents can play a vital role in helping their children meet homework deadlines. Many teenagers, when a deadline has been missed, have a tendency to avoid dealing with the situation. Your role is to encourage them to speak to their teachers and ask for the help that is available at school.

Writing for a teenage audience

When writing for a teenage audience, or for younger children, you should avoid non-standard English, including slang and texting language. However, some carefully used informal language may be appropriate to engage the audience.

Worked example

> **9** Write a speech for a Year 11 assembly giving your views about homework … **(40 marks)**

Let's get things straight. Homework is a pain… and that's putting it mildly. We can all think of much better ways to occupy our time, and frequently many of us do just that! However, if you are behind with your homework, speak to your teacher as soon as you can. After all, they are there to help.

The speech begins with informal figurative language that is appropriate to engage the audience. It is then developed using carefully crafted, more formal language.

Now try this

> **8** Write an article for your school website exploring the importance of GCSE exams … **(40 marks)**

You reckon you've got ages till your GCSEs? You've already bagged a job? I'm telling you, those exams are coming round quick!

Rewrite the opening paragraph of this student answer, using formal Standard English that is more appropriate to the audience.

Putting it into practice

In **Paper 1: Section B – Writing**, you'll need to use your **imaginative writing skills**. Before you start writing, you should think carefully about the question and plan your time.

Planning and checking

How much time should you spend on planning and checking this question in your exam?

For a reminder about the structure of Paper 1: Section B – Writing, go to page 48

Turn to pages 20, 23, 77 and 79 for more about narrative voice and imaginative language techniques

Preparing for imaginative writing

- ✓ Plan your time – you have **45 minutes** for this question, including planning and checking.
- ✓ Read the **questions** carefully.
- ✓ Decide **which question** to answer.
- ✓ **Plan** your writing, including ideas about narrative voice and language techniques.

Look carefully at the exam-style question options below. Think about what each question might involve before you decide which one to answer. Look at one student's thoughts:

EITHER:

5 Write about a time when you, or someone you know, told a lie.
Your response could be real or imagined.
(40 marks)

OR:

6 Look at the images provided.
Write about a deserted house.
Your response could be real or imagined.
You may wish to base your response on one of the images. **(40 marks)**

Both questions are fairly open and don't say which form to use, but I need to write in prose. Neither of the questions specifies a narrative voice, so I can choose which narrative voice to write in, for example, first or third person.

I could choose to write a real personal experience for this question.

Using your own personal experience can be helpful if you find coming up with ideas difficult.

Here, I could use the images provided for inspiration.

Question 6 will appeal to you if you like to visualise your ideas before writing.

Remember that you cannot write a play, a poem or any other type of verse in response to these questions.

Now try this

Look closely at the **Paper 1** exam-style question on the right. You do not need to write an answer. Instead:

- plan your time as if you were in the exam
- read the question carefully, making notes about form and narrative voice
- use a spider diagram or bullet points to get down your initial ideas.

5 Write about a time when you, or someone you know, met a mysterious stranger.
Your response could be real or imagined. **(40 marks)**

Remember that you should allow 10 minutes for the whole planning process, so this task should take you about 5 minutes.

Putting it into practice

In **Paper 2: Section B – Writing**, you'll need to show you can write for **a specific purpose and audience.** Before you start writing, you should think carefully about the questions and plan your time.

Planning and checking

Here is one student's exam plan for this section. Add the missing details.

Timing

Planning: 10 minutes (10.00 – 10.10 am)

Writing: ....

Checking: ....

For a reminder about the structure of Paper 2: Section B – Writing, go to page 49

Preparing for transactional writing

- ✓ Plan your time – you have **45 minutes** to answer the question, including planning and checking.
- ✓ Read the **questions** carefully, decide which question to answer and identify the **topic**.
- ✓ **Annotate** the question to highlight the **form, purpose and audience.**
- ✓ **Plan** your writing.

EITHER

8 Write a guide about your school and local area for a party of visiting American exchange students.

In your guide you could include:

- details about the school, for example, buildings, facilities, catering
- suggestions for what students might study during their visit
- descriptions of local landmarks they might find interesting during their visit

… as well as any other ideas you might have.

(40 marks)

Look carefully at each question on the left and identify exactly what you are being asked to do. Look at how this student has annotated the key features of these questions:

Topic – for example, school life, school day, local attractions

Audience implied – teenagers, but parents might also read

Purpose and form – guides need to inform and explain, use headings/ subheadings

OR

9 Write an article for a newspaper, giving your views about a proposal to raise the driving age to 21 years.

You could write about:

- why young people want, or need, to drive
- the advantages/disadvantages of raising the driving age, for example, safer, older people are more responsible, young people would be less mobile
- your ideas about young people learning to drive

… as well as any other ideas you might have.

(40 marks)

Format – article, needs catchy headline

Implies audience – mainly adults, need formal style

Topic – driving age, advantages/ disadvantages

Implies purpose – to argue/persuade

Now try this

Look closely at the **Paper 2** exam-style question extracts on the right. You do not need to write answers. Instead, draw a four-point spider diagram for each one, to identify the form, purpose, audience and topic.

8 Write a letter to a national newspaper encouraging readers to take part in a campaign to clear up Britain's beaches … **(40 marks)**

9 Write a review of your favourite holiday destination for your local newspaper … **(40 marks)**

Form: articles and reviews

In **Paper 2: Section B – Writing**, you may be asked to write a newspaper or magazine article, or a review. You need to use the key features of the form you are being asked to write in.

Articles

Headline – gives enough information to engage the reader and may use a pun, alliteration, repetition, rhetorical question, etc.

Sub-heading – gives more information, drawing the reader in.

Quotations from experts make the article seem factual and reliable. Note how speech punctuation is used correctly.

The truth about lying: it's the hands that betray you, not the eyes

By analysing videos of liars, the team found there was no link to their eye movements

ADAM SHERWIN

It is often claimed that even the most stone-faced liar will be betrayed by an unwitting eye movement. But new research suggests that 'lying eyes', which no fibber can avoid revealing, are actually a myth. It is actually verbal hesitations and excessive hand gestures that are a better guide.

Prof Wiseman, a psychologist from the University of Hertfordshire, said: 'The results of the first study revealed no relationship between lying and eye movements...'

In the exam you don't need to write the headline in bold block writing or write in columns. Your normal handwriting will do.

Short opening sentence – this introduces the subject and summarises the key points.

Later sentences add more detail.

See page 88 for more about punctuation

Reviews

Title of review – usually catchy to engage the reader and indicate the reviewer's opinion.

Rating – gives a view on how good the film or event is.

Engaging opening paragraph – often uses figurative language to give the reader a taste of what the film or event is like.

Transformers: Age of Extinction, review: *'spectacular junk'*

Much like his shape-shifting robot stars, Michael Bay's pulverising Transformers sequel is cinematic treasure disguised as trash, says Robbie Collin.

★★★☆☆

In Hollywood last week, the skies darkened, the streams ran bitter and a green haze rose from the soil. Strange creatures slunk from the woods, their laughter borne on a foul-smelling wind, and danced horribly while the moon was gibbous.

The new Transformers film, which contains robots that turn into dinosaurs and a weapon that makes people explode, freeze and burst into flames all at the same time, begins with something that is – and there is no other word for it – clever...

Sub-heading – gives more details of the reviewer's opinion.

Further paragraphs add detail and begin to explain the reviewer's opinion.

Note that this structure and organisation is suitable for any type of review. This is for a film, but in the exam you could be asked to review a different kind of consumer item, such as an event, a place or a product.

Now try this

Look at the article and the review on this page. List **three** differences in the features of these two forms.

Form: letters and reports

In **Paper 2: Section B – Writing**, you may also be asked to write a letter or a report.

Letters

Your **address** and the **date** go in the top right-hand corner.

The person you are writing to and their address go on the left, lower down.

Use 'Dear Sir/Madam' if you don't know the name of the person.

Use a **subject line** to draw the reader's immediate attention to your topic – keep the language formal.

Use **Yours faithfully** if you have used 'Dear Sir/Madam'. If you have used the person's name, end with **Yours sincerely**.

57 Woodford Road
Nottingham NG8 4PQ

15 February 2016

The Editor
Nottingham News
17 High Street
Nottingham
NG2 4XY

Dear Sir/Madam

Dog fouling on pavements

It has come to my attention…

and hope that you will take this into account.

Yours faithfully

Jane Smith

Getting it right

In the exam, the most important thing is the quality of your writing. Indicate that it is a letter you are writing – for example, by using 'Dear ...' at the start – but make sure your focus is on the tone and content of your writing. You **do not** need to add addresses in the exam.

Reports

Title – formal and factual.

Introduction – two or three sentences giving the main facts about the topic.

Current situation – says what is happening now.

Recommendation – gives an idea about what should change.

Conclusion – summarises what advantages the proposed change will bring.

School Marathon Events

Most major cities across the world hold marathon events. These events collect thousands of pounds in sponsorship for charities, from the large, well-known national organisations to small, local ones that are personal to the runners.

Our school currently takes part in national events such as Comic Relief and Children in Need. Such events provide the school with an engaging vehicle for teaching a variety of subjects in a way that engages students of all ages. Last year…

However, whilst they are well supported within the school they do not involve the wider community. A school marathon would create an ideal opportunity to reach out…

So a school marathon event would combine two factors that are essential to a well-rounded education: physical activity and the promotion of empathy.

Reports are information texts and should be formal and factual, but you will probably need to give your opinions as part of the recommendations you make.

See page 51 for more about informative writing

Now try this

Look at the letter and report on this page. Which form would be most suitable for the following tasks?

1 An application to join the Royal Air Force.
2 A proposal to install new fitness equipment in the school gym.
3 A thank you note to your elderly grandparents for the present they sent for your recent birthday.

Had a look ☐ Nearly there ☐ Nailed it! ☐

Form: information guides

In **Paper 2: Section B – Writing**, you may be asked to write an information guide.

Headings and sub-headings

Information guides or leaflets are factual and can carry a lot of information. Use headings and sub-headings to guide the reader through the information.

Use adverbials to link your paragraphs and help guide the reader through your points.

See pages 70 and 71 for more about paragraphing and adverbials

Bullet points and numbered lists

Lists can provide a lot of information in a short space. They can also be used to show ranking or a sequence.

Avoid too many bullet points or numbered lists. You need to show you can structure sentences and paragraphs to guide the reader.

Worked example

8 Write a student's guide to your school's behaviour policy.

In your guide you could:

- include examples of school rules
- give details of what can go wrong
- explain what happens if you break the rules

… as well as including any other ideas you might have. **(40 marks)**

High School Academy – Behaviour for Beginners

The rules

High School Academy's behaviour policy works because there are only three very simple rules.

1. Always do your best.
2. Always apologise if you are wrong.
3. Always …

The rules in reality

In reality, there is obviously more to our behaviour policy than just being polite and trying your hardest. Things do go wrong…

Key points to remember

-
-
-

Heading or title – alliteration creates a slightly informal tone suited to the student audience.

Sub-headings structure the text and guide the reader.

A short list – appropriate at the start, but make sure most of your writing shows your skills by using a full variety of sentence structures.

Also see pages 82–84 to revise sentences

Another example of alliteration to engage the audience.

Detailed paragraph with full sentences adds further explanation.

Two or three more sub-headings could be used with a detailed paragraph for each one.

Sub-heading for conclusion – information guides often end with a clear summary of the main points.

Bullet points are used in this conclusion, but you could also use a summary paragraph.

Now try this

Plan your own response to the **Paper 2** exam-style question above. Note down:

- a heading
- four or five key sub-headings
- where you would use lists or paragraphs.

Don't forget to include a sub-heading for the conclusion.

Putting it into practice

Paper 2: Section B – Writing tests your ability to write for **different purposes and audiences**. Read the exam-style question below and the extracts from two students' answers.

Worked example

9 Write an article for a national newspaper exploring the role of teenagers in society.
You could write about:
- the negative way teenagers are viewed by many in society today
- the type of contribution teenagers can make to society, for example, volunteering, mentoring, charity fund-raising
- why teenagers should be encouraged to contribute to society

… as well as any other ideas you might have.

(40 marks)

Transactional writing

For a question like this you should:
- ✓ spend **45 minutes** on your answer, including **planning and checking** time
- ✓ read the **question** carefully and identify the **topic**
- ✓ **annotate** the question to highlight the **form, purpose and audience**
- ✓ **plan** your writing.

Make the purpose of your writing clear in the opening.

Sample answer

Teenagers – humans or hoodlums?

Some teenagers make an effort to contribute to society; 52% of teenagers at our local secondary school have received some form of reward or prize:
- Jane Smith won an art competition
- Alina Bachar helped her neighbour in the garden
- Hamid Zaman won first prize in a National Judo competition.

✓ Catchy headline, appropriate for the audience.

✗ There is no sub-heading to engage the reader or opening paragraph to introduce the subject and purpose (to inform and persuade).

✓ Use of statistics is appropriate for the form and purpose.

✗ Although bullet points can be used in articles, detailed paragraphs would be a better way to establish the key points.

Improved sample answer

Teenagers – dangerous or diligent?

Prejudices are pulled apart as our young people prove their positive impact on society

A regular reader of this newspaper may well feel that all teenagers hang around on street corners, sipping from bottles of alcohol and spitting on passers-by. This image sells newspapers. But is it the whole story?

Positive stories do exist. I know of more teenagers who get it right than wrong. Some readers may choose to buy into the idea that all teenagers are trouble. However, take Alina Bachar, for instance. Rather than idling on street corners, Alina has spent the last year giving up every weekend to help …

✓ Rhetorical question engages the reader.

✓ The sub-heading helps in establishing the subject and purpose.

✓ This developed opening paragraph outlines the subject and gives a clear sense of form and audience.

✓ Developed paragraph details the first key point.

✓ The adverbial 'however' dismisses this well-placed counter-argument.

Now try this

In your own response to the exam-style question above, write:
- a headline
- a sub-heading
- a short opening paragraph
- one developed paragraph about your first key point.

Had a look ☐ Nearly there ☐ Nailed it! ☐

Prose: an overview

The focus of **Paper 1: Section B – Writing** is **imaginative writing**. In the exam, your imaginative writing will need to be in **prose**.

What is prose?

Prose is continuous, paragraphed writing. It is the form often used for narratives (stories), descriptions and monologues, for example. Look at the examples of prose below.

Structuring prose

Whatever you write in response to the imaginative writing question on Paper 1, you must take care to structure your ideas carefully and for effect. Your writing should have a clear beginning, middle and end.

Narrative

This extract from a 19th-century narrative is written in prose.

Extract from The Half-Brothers. *Full text on page 99. Lines 17–20.*

All my youthful hardiness seemed to leave me at once. I was on the point of crying, and only very shame seemed to keep it down. To save myself from shedding tears, I shouted—terrible, wild shouts for bare life they were. I turned sick as I paused to listen; no answering sound came but the unfeeling echoes.

Getting it right

In the exam, the Paper 1 writing questions will not tell you which form your writing should take. However:

✓ you should write in prose

✗ you should not write a poem

✗ you should not write a play.

Dialogue

Narratives can include dialogue, like this example from the 19th century.

Extract from The Adventures of Tom Sawyer. *Full text on page 98. Lines 13–16.*

"Tom!"

"Well, Becky?"

"They'll miss us and hunt for us!"

"Yes, they will! Certainly they will!"

However, avoid too much dialogue in your imaginative writing; focus instead on full paragraphs of prose.

Description

Prose is also the form used for description. Here is an example from the 19th century.

Extract from Little Dorrit. *Full text on page 96. Lines 32–36.*

He had a hook nose, handsome after its kind, but too high between the eyes by probably just as much as his eyes were too near to one another. For the rest, he was large and tall in frame, had thin lips, where his thick moustache showed them at all, and a quantity of dry hair, of no definable colour, in its shaggy state, but shot with red.

Monologue

Monologues are written in prose, too.

Well, frankly I still can't believe his nerve. I asked him, quite directly, where the cake had gone and he stared at me, eyes like saucers, as though I'd recently descended to Earth from an extremely distant and hitherto undiscovered planet. It's not a difficult question, after all, and I'm still waiting for an answer. Pointing at the dog, which he did, is hardly fair, after all. I mean, I ask you!

Now try this

Answer the following questions using the information on this page.

1 What form should your imaginative writing take in the exam?

2 Name two forms that you should avoid in the exam.

Ideas and planning: imaginative

For **Paper 1: Section B – Writing** you will need to produce a piece of **imaginative writing**. Planning is the best way to produce a well-structured and fully developed piece of writing.

Question options

You will be given **two question options** for the writing task in **Paper 1**. For example:

EITHER

5 Write about a time when you, or someone you know, helped others.
Your response could be real or imagined.
(40 marks)

OR

6 Look at images C and D on page 106.
Write about an unusual journey.
Your response could be real or imagined. You may wish to base your response on one of the images.
(40 marks)

Remember: you do not have to use the images for Question 6 if you prefer not to.

Turn to page 48 to refresh your memory about Paper 1: Section B – Writing

Ideas – picturing it

Picture the scene or event in your mind (or look at the images provided if you have decided to answer Question 6).
Ask yourself:

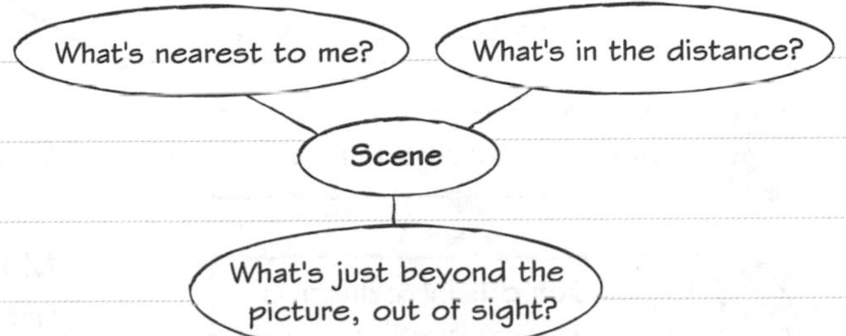

Ideas – what's happening?

Think about the characters and action:

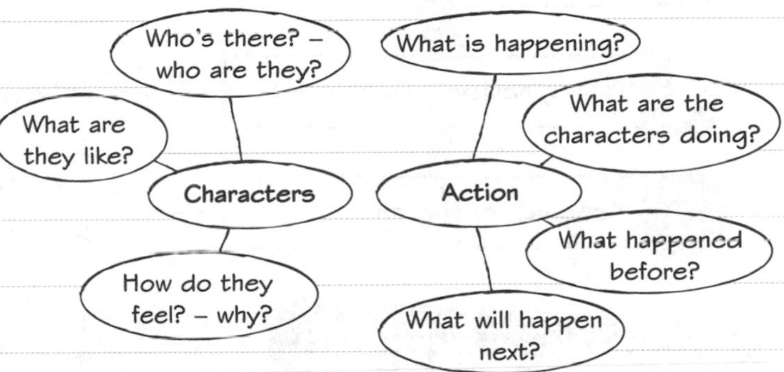

Getting it right

- Spend around **10 minutes planning**.
- **Choose the question** you are going to answer as quickly as you can. Which do you have the most initial ideas about?
- Think about which **narrative voice** to use. If you write about an event that you have experienced yourself, use the first person.
- **Stay focused** on the question topic.
- Plan ideas for **four or five paragraphs**.
- Include ideas for **imaginative writing techniques**.

Turn to pages 77–79 for more about imaginative writing techniques

Planning

Plans can take various forms. A **spider diagram** keeps your ideas centred around the **main idea in the question**:

Recall conversation with old man, use dialogue to show character

When I helped others – volunteering at homeless shelter, real experience, first person narrative

Queues at mealtimes, use five senses to bring scene to life

Now try this

Choose one of the **Paper 1** exam-style questions above. Gather and plan ideas for four or five paragraphs.

You have 10 minutes in total to plan your answer for this type of question, so this task should take about 5 minutes.

Had a look ☐ Nearly there ☐ Nailed it! ☐

Structure: imaginative

For **Paper 1: Section B – Writing** you will need to structure your **imaginative writing** effectively. The best way to achieve this is to use some type of **narrative** structure.

Narrative structure

In the exam, you are most likely to write a short story. Short stories work best when they use a simple five-part structure like this:

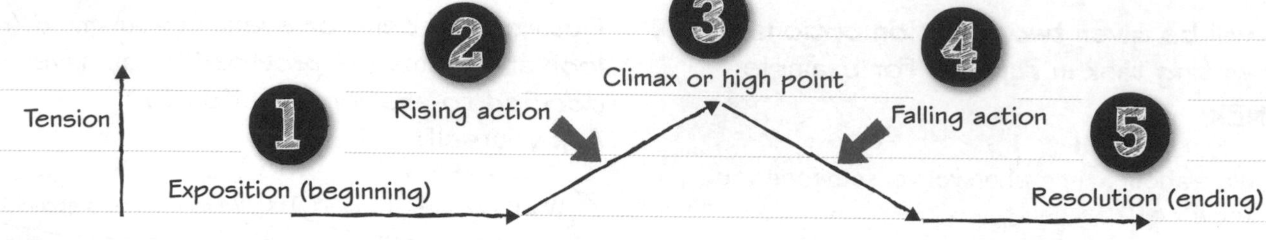

1 **Exposition:** the beginning — Characters and setting established.

2 **Rising action:** introduction of problem or conflict — Main problem or conflict introduced and dealt with by some kind of action. This is the place for tension and excitement.

3 **Climax:** the high point — The main event or danger faced by the character or characters.

4 **Falling action:** winding down — Following the climax, the story begins to wind down.

5 **Resolution:** the ending — Conflicts are resolved, all loose ends are tied up and the story concludes on a happy or a sad note.

You could play with the narrative structure, starting at the climax and using flashbacks to the exposition and rising action.

Worked example

5 Write about a time when you, or someone you know, had to change your plans.
Your response could be real or imagined.
(40 marks)

Exposition: Woke up – excited – day out with boyfriend.

Rising action: Boyfriend phoned – finished with me. Mum tells me to stop sulking and help her at homeless shelter.

Climax: Meet mysterious stranger at homeless shelter.

Falling action: Get to know his story.

Resolution: Start working at homeless shelter.

✓ A clear narrative structure – each point can be expanded into more detailed paragraphs.

Now try this

Use this five-part narrative structure to **plan** an answer to this **Paper 1** exam-style question.

5 Write about a time when you, or someone you know, won a prize.
Your response could be real or imagined.
(40 marks)

Remember to plan where you will use appropriate imaginative writing techniques.

Beginnings and endings: imaginative

The **beginning** and **ending** of a piece of **imaginative writing** are very important. Both need to have an **impact** on the reader.

The beginning

This needs to:

- engage the reader immediately
- set the tone for the rest of your writing.

You can do this with: a vivid description, dialogue, a mystery, or conflict or danger.

The beginning is sometimes called the 'exposition' or 'opening'.

With a vivid description

Glistening and gleaming in the evening haze, the sea spread out before us like a silver carpet. Waves lapped gently at the sides of the boat as we sailed silently along in the cool, salty breeze.

A good way to start if the setting plays a big role in your writing.

Opportunities to show your skills with imaginative writing techniques like figurative language.

With dialogue

'I'm scared. What do we do now?' Shadows flickered on Sarah's terrified face as she whispered her fears.

'Nothing,' he hissed. 'Keep quiet and just wait.'

Gives the reader an immediate idea about one or more important characters

With a mystery

I know I shouldn't have taken it. But I did. I'll be sorry for the rest of my miserable little life. It was only a tiny thing – but it caused so much trouble.

An engaging way to start if you want to use flashbacks.

Go to page 62 for more about narrative structure and flashbacks

With conflict or danger

I froze. Someone was in the house. I couldn't see them. But I knew they were there.

An effective way to create a sense of tension from the start.

The ending

The ending is the final impression the reader has of your writing. Follow these rules for a strong ending:

- **plan** each stage of your writing in advance – you will be less likely to run out of time and rush at the end
- spend time thinking about the **tone** of your ending – will it be happy, sad or funny?
- craft your **final sentence** carefully – this is the last bit of your writing an examiner will read
- avoid sudden mood changes – if the tone of your writing has been tense throughout, a happy ending is unlikely to work
- avoid ending with a cliché like 'it was all a dream' – use your imagination!

Now try this

Look at this **Paper 1** exam-style question, then answer the questions below.

> **5** Write about a time when you, or someone you know, were at home alone.
> Your response could be real or imagined.
> **(40 marks)**

1 Write four possible openings using the techniques on this page. Use a different technique for each opening.

2 Choose one of your openings and write the final paragraph.

Had a look ☐ Nearly there ☐ Nailed it! ☐

Putting it into practice

Paper 1: Section B – Writing tests your **imaginative writing** skills. Planning before you write will help you to produce a stronger answer. Look at the exam-style question below and the two students' plans.

Worked example

5 Write about a time you, or someone you know, had an unexpected visitor.
Your response could be real or imagined. **(40 marks)**

Planning for imaginative writing

To plan for a question like this you should:

- ✓ spend **10 minutes planning** your answer – the more detailed your plan is, the stronger your answer will be
- ✓ quickly decide **which question** to answer
- ✓ **plan** the narrative voice and imaginative writing techniques you will use
- ✓ create a **full and detailed plan.**

Sample plan

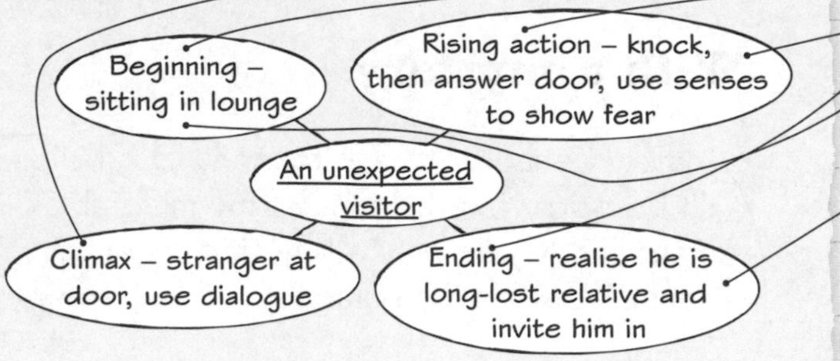

An unexpected visitor
- Beginning – sitting in lounge
- Rising action – knock, then answer door, use senses to show fear
- Climax – stranger at door, use dialogue
- Ending – realise he is long-lost relative and invite him in

✓ Clear use of narrative structure.
✗ Details too brief in places and lack notes on imaginative writing techniques.
✗ Ending happens too suddenly.

Note how the narrative structure does not include a 'falling action' section. This may lead to the narrative feeling rushed at the end.

Improved sample plan

Heading:	An unexpected visitor
Climax:	start with mystery – fear when door is opened and nobody there; create mysterious atmosphere with short sentence
Exposition:	flashback using description of setting before knock on door, use senses to show calm feelings
Rising action:	knock on door, use metaphor for feelings
Climax:	reveal who is at door, stranger who hands over a package and then leaves, package has 'do not open' written on front; use personification of package to create tension
Falling action:	describe examining the package and then finding, on the back 'until the morning'...
Resolution:	end by ...

Go back to page 50 to revise the basics of imaginative writing techniques

✓ Detailed use of narrative structure, using flashback to engage the reader.
✓ Detailed plan with notes about techniques to be used at each stage of the narrative.
✓ Ending is planned after full 'wind down' to fully engage reader.

Now try this

Finish the 'Improved sample plan' by adding more detail to the 'falling action' and adding an appropriate ending for the narrative. Note down your ideas for **imaginative writing techniques** you could use for the falling action and ending sections. Then write the first **two paragraphs** of an answer using this plan. Use one or more of the techniques for beginnings and endings from page 63.

Ideas and planning: inform, explain, review

Paper 2: Section B – Writing tests your skills in writing for **different audiences and purposes**. Planning your answer will help you to choose the **form, features** and **techniques** that best suit the task's **audience** and **purpose**.

Plan an introduction that says what you are writing about and why it is important.

You will need three or four **key points**. These should be your main ideas.

Add ideas to each of your key points. You may decide to combine two key points in one paragraph, or divide one key point into two paragraphs.

Use temporal (time) adverbials to guide your reader through your points.

Use **appropriate techniques** to support the **audience and purpose**.

Worked example

8 Write a report for your local council about the facilities available in your area for teenagers.

In your report you could:

- state what is available at the moment for teenagers
- suggest how current facilities could be improved
- explain what new facilities are needed and what the benefits would be

… as well as including any other ideas you might have. **(40 marks)**

Plan

Introduction

- Firstly… not enough facilities
- need to improve them
- stop teenagers causing problems in town – could include statistics of recent trouble

1 Key point – **Existing facilities**

- facts – what is available now
- poor condition – give example of astro-turf & use expert opinion

2 Key point – **Improvements suggested**

- youth club – redecorate, could ask teenagers to help?
- repair astro-turf, get grant from sports company
- add computers to local library

3 Key point – **New facilities**

- bowling alley, give an estimate of how much money this could bring in
- coffee shop – could be run by volunteers

Conclusion

- Finally… explain benefit to other local people

You might want to change the order of your paragraphs once you have written your plan.

Getting it right

Remember:

- you have **45 minutes** to complete **the task**
- you should spend **10 minutes planning**
- your plan should include appropriate techniques for the purpose
- use the bullet points in the question to help with ideas.

Now try this

Look at this Paper 2 exam-style question and plan an answer.

9 Write a guide for parents explaining what they can do to help their children with the stress of exams.

You could write about:

- what causes the stress and how teenagers feel when stressed
- what practical help parents can give, for example, ensuring their children eat properly and take breaks
- where parents could go to get support and advice

… as well as any other ideas you might have. **(40 marks)**

Think carefully about the structure and the features and techniques you need to include to suit the audience and purpose.

Ideas and planning: argue and persuade

Planning is the only way to produce a well-structured piece of writing, full of relevant imaginative ideas and carefully crafted language. It will help you to **structure** your **transactional writing** for **Paper 2: Section B – Writing** in a logical way that helps the reader to follow your ideas.

Worked example

8 Write a speech for a school assembly, giving your views about whether television is a waste of time … **(40 marks)**

Plan: TV is stealing your life

Intro
100s of channels run all day and all night
Average person watches 4 hours a day – a quarter of their waking life!

1 TV is passive not active
Evidence: my sister – hours spent staring, doing nothing.
Overweight and silent, her brain and body are being killed by TV.

2 TV is addictive
Once you start, it's difficult to turn off.
Evidence: watch whatever is on, not choosing what to watch.

~~Advertising is annoying~~
~~10/15 mins of it every hour – they want my money!~~

3 Families don't talk any more
Evidence: Mine eats dinner in silence in front of the telly.

4 Some say it's educational and entertaining
It can be both – but how often? More often it's neither – e.g. Big Brother.

Conclusion
Most telly is a waste of time for everyone.
Choose what you want to watch – then turn it off.

You could choose to give a balanced view, or to focus more on one side of the subject.

Don't be afraid to cross out some of your ideas.

Write your introduction, telling the reader what the situation is at the moment, and why that is a problem they need to think about.

Add some evidence to support each key point you make. **Plan key points** by gathering together all the different ideas you can think of that support your viewpoint.

Choose and sequence the most persuasive points. You will probably only need two or three key points.

Don't stop when you've thought of three ideas. Think of more, reject weaker ideas, then put the strong ideas in a logical order.

Add a counter-argument that gives an opposing viewpoint. Then say why you disagree.

Plan a conclusion – your final point to hammer home your argument.

Now try this

The plan above gives the view that television **is** a waste of time. Write a new plan in response to the exam-style question, giving the view that television **is not** a waste of time.

Openings: transactional

Starting a piece of writing can be difficult. For **Paper 2: Section B – Writing**, know what you want to write, or you will be in danger of writing one or two boring paragraphs before you really get going.

An effective opening

Your first paragraph of any writing task – and your first sentence in particular – needs to grab the reader's interest and attention. You could use one or more of these five ideas.

- A bold and / or controversial statement:

> Experimenting on animals is a cruel necessity.

- A relevant quotation:

> 'What's in a name? That which we call a rose by any other name would smell as sweet.'
>
> (William Shakespeare, *Romeo and Juliet*, 2.2)

- A shocking or surprising fact or statistic:

> 99 per cent of the species that have ever lived on Planet Earth are now extinct.

- A rhetorical question:

> How many of us can honestly say that we care more about others than we do about ourselves?

- A short, relevant, **interesting** anecdote:

> When I was seven, my parents bought me a dog. This was when I first realised that ...

Getting it right

- Avoid telling the reader what you are going to write about:

In this essay I am going to argue that television is not a waste of time.

Just write it:

Television is informative, educational and interesting.

Introducing your topic

After your opening sentence, go on to introduce what you are writing about.

> ... The average person spends a quarter of their waking life watching television. Are they making good use of their time? Or is television sucking the life out of them, killing them slowly with its mind-numbing mediocrity?

A surprising statistic shocks the reader and grabs their attention. Here, it invites the reader to compare how long they spend watching TV.

Two questions engage the reader, and present the two sides of the argument. The second question makes it clear which side the writer is on.

Now try this

> **9** Write an article for a newspaper, exploring the benefits a skateboard ramp would bring to the local park ...
>
> **(40 marks)**

Look at the **Paper 2** exam-style question extract opposite.

1 Write **three** possible openings that would engage your reader's attention from the start.

2 Choose the most effective opening, then complete the introduction.

Had a look ☐ Nearly there ☐ Nailed it! ☐

Conclusions: transactional

For **Paper 2: Section B – Writing**, plan your conclusion before you start writing. Your final paragraph should leave your reader with a lasting impression.

Summing up

Plan your conclusion before you start writing. The final paragraph or conclusion to a text can be used to sum up your ideas – but avoid repeating them. Instead, aim to sum up and emphasise your central idea. You could use one or more of these things.

Look back over your writing and consider how you might sum it up neatly and leave your reader with a clear message.

End on a vivid image: a picture that lingers in the reader's mind. A homeless person sits cold and alone in a shop doorway. As you pass by, you look into her eyes. She can't be older than 15.	**End on a warning:** what will happen if your ideas are not acted on? Within 50 years, the world will have changed beyond all recognition – and our children will blame us for what has happened.	**End on a happy note:** emphasise how great things will be if your ideas are acted on. Ours could be the generation that made the difference.
End on a thought-provoking question: leave the reader thinking. For how long can we ignore what is staring us in the face?	**Refer back to your introduction**, but don't repeat it. I still have that dog – and he's still incredibly badly behaved. But if I hadn't …	**End on a call to action:** make it clear what you want the reader to do. Don't just sit there. Get up, get out and make it happen.

Worked example

Remember that questions engage the reader with the issue – how does it relate to their own life?

8 Write an article for a national newspaper giving your views about whether television is a waste of time ...

(40 marks)

How many hours of television have you watched this week? What else could you have done with those hours? Television has turned us all into spectators – and while we're glued to the box, <u>our lives are ticking away, wasted and unused.</u> It's time to stop watching. <u>It's time to start taking part.</u>

A warning.

A final, powerful call to action.

This is an example of a conclusion.

Now try this

Look at the **Paper 2** exam-style question extract opposite.
Choose **one or more** of the above techniques to write a powerful conclusion.

9 Write an article for a newspaper, exploring the benefits a skateboard ramp would bring to the local park …

(40 marks)

Putting it into practice

Paper 2: Section B – Writing tests your skills in writing for **different audiences and purposes**. Planning before you write will help you produce stronger answers. Look at the exam-style question below and the two students' plans.

Worked example

9 Write a review of a popular tourist attraction in your local area for your community magazine.

You could write about:

- an attraction such as a museum, theme park or historical site
- what facilities the attraction offers for visitors, for example, food available, children's rides/parks, visitor centre
- why it is popular, for example, its history

… as well as any other ideas you might have.

(40 marks)

Remember to read the bullet points carefully; they may help you with your ideas and planning.

Planning for transactional writing

To plan for a question like this you should:

- spend **10 minutes planning** your answer – the more detailed your plan is, the stronger your answer will be
- **annotate** the question to highlight the **form, purpose** and **audience**
- **plan** the features and techniques you will use to support the **form, purpose** and **audience**
- create a **full and detailed plan**.

Sample plan

Bradcaster Park

- Good, fun, interesting.
- Playground for kids.
- Lake
-

✓ Some language ideas but undeveloped / unambitious.

✓ Some ideas gathered, but more needed.

Make sure you provide a range of details for questions like this. In this plan there is no detail added about the lake, the information about the park is not sequenced, and there is no introduction or conclusion.

Improved sample plan

Goose Fair: 700 years of family fun!

1. Intro: use an anecdote about first visit

2. History: origins as animal market

3. Popularity: use statistics about visitor numbers, number of rides & position as top attraction in Nottm

4. What is there? Rides/food – describe with similes and personification

Conclusion: go back to intro – latest visit still as good

✓ Features – title and sub-headings – are appropriate for a review.

✓ Ideas sequenced into a logical structure.

✓ Detail added.

✓ Plans made for opening and conclusion.

This student has used a spider diagram but the bullet point planning form used on page 65 would work just as well. It is the detail in the planning that is important, not the style of the plan.

Now try this

Plan your answer to the above exam-style question and write an opening paragraph.

Remember to:

- gather, organise and sequence your ideas
- plan your introduction and conclusion.

Had a look ☐ Nearly there ☐ Nailed it! ☐

Paragraphing for effect

The best answers are organised into **paragraphs**. They help **structure** your writing, making it easier for the reader to follow your thinking and absorb your ideas. You will need to use paragraphs for your writing in **both papers**.

Paragraphing for effect

In most cases you should start a new paragraph each time you start a new point. However, you can use shorter paragraphs for effect: to emphasise a point or create a dramatic pause.

A one-sentence paragraph can create a sense of tension and pace. Here, it leaves the reader in suspense about what actually happens to Ben. This will make them want to continue reading.

one paragraph = one point

> Settling in front of the fire, Ben kicked off his shoes and stretched out his toes towards the warmth. Outside, rain battered the windows, through which he could just make out the autumn leaves as they danced around the garden and settled on the surface of the pond. Today was a good day to stay inside and relax.
>
> Later, Ben was to see that moment as his last real taste of freedom.
>
> The day had started much like any other. He had eaten his cereal, brushed his teeth, checked his bag and then left for school.

Structuring paragraphs: argue and persuade

Use Point-Evidence-Explanation to structure paragraphs in a piece of writing to argue or persuade.

- A short, clear **point**.
- **Evidence** to support the point.
- **Explains** how the point and evidence are relevant to the main idea.

> Britain's weather is changing. Barely a month goes by without it being declared the wettest, the driest, the hottest, the coldest, or the windiest month on record. Our weather is clearly becoming more extreme, and is likely to become even more so. How long can we ignore this before we act?

Structuring paragraphs: inform, explain, review

Start each paragraph with a **topic sentence** – a sentence that clearly introduces the reader to the content of this paragraph. Use the remainder of the paragraph to develop and add detail to the topic sentence.

- Topic sentence
- Detail / development

> Our school has made a huge effort to recycle its waste. Every classroom has a bin just for waste paper, which is collected each week by student volunteers. In the canteen, we sort our rubbish into plastics, tin cans, and food waste. Even the staff room has three different bins so teachers can recycle!

Now try this

Write one paragraph in response to this Paper 2 exam-style question:

> **9** Write a report for your school's head of catering on the quality of food on offer in the school canteen … **(40 marks)**

Linking ideas

Adverbials can be used to **guide** the reader through your ideas. They can work like **signposts**, showing the reader the direction your ideas are taking. Use adverbials to improve your writing for **both papers**.

Adding an idea

- Moreover ...
- Furthermore ...
- In addition ...

This will not solve the situation. **Moreover**, it could make it worse.

Furthermore, this is likely to interrupt students' learning and add to their stress levels.

Explaining

- As a result
- Therefore
- Consequently

Science suggests that the teenage brain needs more sleep to help it grow and develop. **Consequently**, we spend longer in bed.

Teenagers' attitudes and actions are constantly challenged. It is **therefore** unsurprising that they sometimes challenge those who challenge them.

Illustrating

- For example
- For instance

For example, teenagers are frequently assumed to be responsible for graffiti and vandalism.

Emphasising

- In particular
- Especially
- Significantly

Significantly, these problems increased when the youth club was shut down.

Time or **temporal** adverbials are very useful for indicating the passage of time in creative writing.

Comparing and contrasting

Comparing	**Contrasting**
Similarly	However
Likewise	On the other hand
In the same way	On the contrary

It has been argued that an animal's life is not as valuable as that of a human being. **Similarly**, some have said that animals exist only because humans need them as a source of food. **However**, I would like to stress that...

Showing time

- Afterwards
- At this moment
- Before
- Previously
- After a while
- Then
- Later
- Meanwhile

Immediately **afterwards** he was to wonder what all the fuss had been about. **After a while** he was even able to see that he had dramatically over-reacted. But at the point when the door swung open, Ben had no thought in his head beyond...

Now try this

Read this student's writing. Add a range of adverbials to link the ideas together and guide the reader through them.

This morning, my sister proved that she is the most annoying person on earth. She finished all the milk so there was none left for me. She spent an hour in the bathroom. She borrowed my headphones without asking and wouldn't give them back. She can be thoughtful. She made me a delicious lasagne the other day. She always remembers my birthday and buys me great presents.

Putting it into practice

For **both papers**, you need to structure your writing in a way that makes it easy for the reader to follow. Using paragraphs and adverbials will help you to do this. Look at the **Paper 2** exam-style question below and then read the extracts from two students' answers.

Worked example

9 Write an article for your local newspaper encouraging older people to discover more about the benefits of modern technology.

You could write about:

- what types of technology they could use
- how the technology will make their lives easier
- where to get help with modern technology

… as well as any other ideas you might have. **(40 marks)**

Paragraphing and adverbials

For each writing question you should:

- ✓ write in paragraphs
- ✓ plan one developed point per paragraph
- ✓ use adverbials to guide your reader through the text.

Sample answer extract

One of the most popular things you can do on the internet is social networking. You can go on websites like Facebook and keep in touch with all your friends. You can also use online encyclopedias to find out about anything you want to know. You can also use the internet to save your photos and share them with your friends and relatives on websites like Facebook, which links back to what I was saying before.

✓ A clear point supported with evidence.

✗ This evidence should be supported with a persuasive explanation.

✗ This point should have been sequenced to develop the first point, using an adverbial to guide the reader.

Remember that a new point should mean a new paragraph. Remember also to support your points with evidence or an explanation. This point contains neither.

Improved sample answer

The internet is a modern miracle: a world of information at your fingertips, waiting to be discovered. Thanks to clever websites called 'search engines', all you have to do is type in a few words and up will pop an enormous choice of websites, all ready to tell you what you want to know. It's so simple, you'll be surfing the internet before you know it.

There are hundreds of things you can do on a computer as well as accessing the internet. For example, you can email friends and relations around the world, sharing your news and views in just a few clicks. It's much quicker than writing a letter – and you don't have to pay a fortune for a stamp, so it can even save you money.

✓ Paragraph clearly organised using:

- point
- evidence
- explanation.

Note the accurate paragraphing with links back to the previous paragraph and also the adverbial (For example) to introduce evidence.

Getting it right

Remember:

- write in paragraphs
- use P-E-E to structure your paragraphs
- use adverbials to link your paragraphs and guide the reader through your ideas.

Now try this

Plan and write the next **two** paragraphs of the 'Improved sample answer' above. Use the bullet points in the question to help you with ideas.

Vocabulary for effect: synonyms

Synonyms are words with similar meanings. Use them in your writing for **both papers** to avoid repetition and to add variety.

Using synonyms can make your writing more varied and interesting. Having a range of synonyms for key words and ideas in mind as you write will mean that:

- you don't repeat the same key word throughout your writing
- you can pick the most precise word – the one that really says what you want it to say.

Be your own thesaurus

You know hundreds – perhaps thousands – of words that you rarely use. So you don't need a thesaurus to come up with ambitious, effective vocabulary chosen for its impact. You just need to think through your mental thesaurus. Beware though! Don't use a word if you are not absolutely sure of its precise meaning.

Examples of synonyms

Comments on evidence often involve the phrase This suggests … Replace it with:

- This gives the impression that …
- It seems clear that …
- This implies …
- In other words …

Arguments are often about ideas. To avoid repeating the word idea, you could use:

- notion
- point
- concept
- opinion
- viewpoint

Worked example

9 Write a speech for a school assembly, giving your views on whether or not celebrities make good role models for young people …

(40 marks)

The idea of celebrities as perfect role models is not the only misguided idea connected with the world of the celebrity. Some people have the idea that celebrities should be consulted on everything from international politics to haircare.

Repetition can add pace and rhythm to your writing – but there are too many words being repeated too often here, weakening an otherwise strong paragraph.

Getting it right

Using the same word more than once can undo all the hard word you put into an answer, making your ideas seem repetitive and uninteresting.

Now try this

Before you start, make a list of all the synonyms you can think of for the word 'celebrity'. You can use a thesaurus if you get stuck.

Rewrite the 'Worked example answer' opposite, replacing the words 'celebrities', 'celebrity' and 'idea' with different synonyms.

Had a look ☐ Nearly there ☐ Nailed it! ☐

Vocabulary for effect: argue and persuade

When writing to **argue or persuade** in **Paper 2: Section B – Writing**, you need to be able to use a wide vocabulary of **emotive words** and **positive and negative language**.

Vocabulary for impact

Using emotive language can add impact to your argument. For example, you may think that global warming is a problem. To shock your reader into action, you want to emphasise the problem by choosing a more emotive word:

If we ignore global warming now, we will soon be facing a ~~problem.~~

catastrophe. | disaster. | calamity.

Add even more power to your sentence by intensifying the emotive word:

horrific | alarming | terrifying

we will soon be facing a catastrophe. terrifying

Positive and negative

If you frame your ideas in **positive** or **negative** language you can control your reader's reaction to them. For example:

If you **support** fox hunting, it could be described as: 'A humane method of pest control'.

If you **oppose** fox hunting, it could be described as: 'A cruel and barbaric sport'.

If you are arguing in **support** of typical teenage behaviour, you could point out that: 'Sleep is an essential ingredient for the teenage brain's development.'

Taking the **opposing point of view** you might write: 'Idle teenagers lounge in bed for hours, paralysed by their crippling laziness.'

Connotations

You can guide your reader's reaction by thinking about the connotations of your vocabulary choice. Look at these words. Each one has a similar meaning but carries different associations.

Six hours of intensive revision can make you

- exhausted. — extreme, intense
- drained. — implies weak, empty
- sleepy. — sounds childish, mocking

Fox hunting is

- brutal. — emphasises violence
- barbaric. — suggests uncivilised
- heartless. — emphasises lack of feeling or empathy

Now try this

Look at the **Paper 2** exam-style question extract on the right. Decide whether you agree or disagree with the idea in the question, then write the opening paragraph of your answer, focusing on vocabulary to argue and persuade.

9 Write an article for a school newspaper, exploring the idea that school is cruel …
(40 marks)

Remember to choose vocabulary for its impact and for its connotations.

Language for different effects 1

Language techniques can add **power** and **impact** to your writing. These techniques will mainly be useful for your transactional writing for **Paper 2**, but you could also use them in your imaginative writing for **Paper 1**.

Rhetorical questions

Use these in argument or persuasive writing to lead the reader to the answer you want.

There is really only one way to answer these questions:

> Who in their right mind would do such a thing?

> Would you stand by and do nothing if you saw a human being treated like this?

You can also use them in creative writing to engage the reader in a situation:

> What was going on?

> What should I do?

Contrast

Place two opposing ideas or situations in direct contrast to emphasise the difference.

> You can work hard in a job you hate for the rest of your life

> or you can work hard on your GCSEs for a couple of years and get the job you want.

You can also use contrast in creative writing to exaggerate a detail: 'Among all the smiling, happy faces there was just one exception: my father's sour-faced, snarling scowl.'

Repetition

Repeating a word or phrase can emphasise a key point or idea in an argument:

> Chasing a helpless animal across open country is cruel. Setting a pack of dogs on a helpless animal is cruel. Watching as the dogs butcher the helpless animal is cruel.

It can also add emphasis to an idea in creative writing:

> There is no point in discussing it, there is no point in arguing about it, there is no point in shouting about it. Once my father has made up his mind, it is made up.

Lists

Use a list to suggest a range of ideas in your persuasive writing:

> It's quick, simple, easy and cheap.

> The improvement would be huge: students would learn more, learn faster, be more motivated, enjoy school more and achieve better results.

Use it to suggest range or variety in your descriptive writing.

> Scattered across the carpet were balloons, paper hats, lumps of cake, streamers and torn shreds of wrapping paper.

Now try this

Choose **one** of these exam-style questions.

Paper 1:

> **5** Write about a time when you, or someone you know, visited a favourite place.
> Your response could be real or imagined.
> **(40 marks)**

Paper 2:

> **9** Write an article for your school newspaper, encouraging more students to take up sport …
> **(40 marks)**

Write **four** short extracts in response to your chosen question. Use **one** of the language techniques above in each extract.

Read a wide variety of fiction and non-fiction texts and note how professional writers use these techniques.

Language for different effects 2

Language techniques can add **power** and **impact** to your writing. These techniques will mainly be useful for your transactional writing for **Paper 2**, but you could also use them in your imaginative writing for **Paper 1**.

Direct address

For **Paper 2: Section B – Writing** questions, talking directly to the reader can be very persuasive.

'**you** can get involved in lots of different ways'

This involves the reader and is much more persuasive than:

'There are many ways to get involved.'

Using the **first person plural 'we'** can create a relationship between you, the writer, and the reader. It suggests that we are all in the same situation, facing the same problems:

'If **we** do nothing, then nothing will change. It is up to us to act and act now.'

Pattern of three

Putting words or phrases in linked groups of three adds rhythm and emphasis to your ideas in all kinds of writing:

It doesn't matter if you're a beginner, an improver, or an expert. It's fun for everyone!

It will benefit the students, the teachers, and the community as a whole.

I approached the front door. My hands were cold, clammy and shaking.

Alliteration

Alliteration can add rhythm and emphasis to your writing. Remember: the alliterative words do not have to be *next* to each other – just *near* each other.

It was a truly terrifying experience.

Combined with other language techniques, alliteration can be particularly engaging and powerful: 'It's fun, fast and furious.'

Hyperbole

Exaggeration can:

- add humour to an argument or a description:

The house looked like a herd of elephants had run through it, detonating hand grenades as they went.

- emphasise a key point:

Teachers want their students to sit completely still and in total silence for six hours a day.

Now try this

Choose **one** of these exam-style questions. Write **four** short extracts in response to your chosen question, using **one** of the language techniques above in each extract.

Paper 1:

5 Write about a time when you, or someone you know, felt under pressure.
Your response could be real or imagined. **(40 marks)**

Paper 2:

8 Write a letter to your local MP, giving your views on a government proposal to prevent under-16s owning a mobile phone … **(40 marks)**

Language for different effects 3

You can use **figurative language** to create powerful images in your readers' minds. You should certainly use figurative language in your **imaginative writing** for **Paper 1**. If you use it carefully (and not too often), figurative language can also show your originality in the **transactional writing tasks** in **Paper 2**.

Similes

A simile is a comparison, usually using **as** or **like**, suggesting a resemblance between one thing and another. It can be used:

- **to inform**

When you get it right, skateboarding can be as exhilarating as a skydive from 30,000 feet.

- **to persuade**

Smoking cigarettes is like a game of Russian roulette – and the chances are, you'll end up losing.

Metaphors

A metaphor is a direct comparison suggesting a resemblance between one thing and another. It can be used:

- **to argue**

At night, when there is nothing else to do, the youth club is a bright light in the darkness, drawing all the young people of the town through its doors.

- **to describe**

She stared and stared, her eyes burning holes in my face.

Personification

Personification is the technique of describing something non-human as if it were human. It can be used when writing:

- **to describe**

Sunlight danced on the water as we headed out to sea.

- **to persuade**

Smoking is highly addictive and, once the habit has got its hands around your throat, it will not let go.

Getting it right

- **Don't** try to force one simile, one metaphor **and** one personification into each answer.
- **Do** use figurative language in your transactional writing for **Paper 2**, but **don't** overdo it.
- **Do** look for opportunities where figurative language will add impact to your ideas.
- **Do** avoid clichés – try to be original.

Avoiding clichés

While an imaginative and original simile or metaphor can add greatly to your writing, a cliché can destroy the effect. So **do not** describe someone as:

- cool as a cucumber
- white as a sheet
- blind as a bat

... or any other comparison that your reader will have read many times before.

Now try this

Choose **one** of these exam-style questions. Write three short extracts in response to your chosen questions. Use one of the language techniques above in each extract.

Paper 1:

5 Write about a time when you, or someone you know, met a hero.
Your response could be real or imagined. **(40 marks)**

Paper 2:

9 Write an article for your local newspaper, exploring the idea that, in today's society, children grow up too fast ... **(40 marks)**

Using the senses

Using **the five senses** is one of the techniques you can use to **develop** your ideas and **engage** the reader, particularly in your **imaginative prose writing**. You might also use the senses in some transactional writing, for example, a travel review.

The five senses

The five senses are: **sight**, **sound**, **touch**, **taste** and **smell**. Use all the five senses (not just sight):

- when you describe a place or an experience
- to make your descriptions vivid
- to engage the reader
- to help the reader to imagine they are there
- to help your writing to stand out.

This sentence uses descriptive language to create an image:

He could see that the fridge was crammed to the top with mouldy, stinking food that looked as if it was at least two years past its sell-by date.

Try to **show, not tell.** A paragraph starting 'he saw', followed by 'then he smelt' and 'later he touched' is unlikely to engage the reader.

These carefully chosen adjectives **show** the reader.

This **tells** the reader with the words 'he could see'.

Careful choice of verbs and descriptive detail shows rather than tells the reader about what is seen and felt.

An adverb is used to intensify this use of the sense of sight.

Clever use of sense of smell avoids telling the reader 'The fridge smelled very bad'.

Notice how this extract is more engaging and powerful because the senses of smell and touch are used to add detail.

He recoiled from the fridge door as the fumes assaulted his nostrils. Had somebody actually died in there? Peering cautiously in it was obvious that every corner was crammed with mouldy, stinking food that looked as if it was at least two years past its sell-by date. His fingers brushed against something soft and furry buried in the door. The source of the fumes – something that hadn't actually been milk since the last century.

Now try this

This plan describes a kitchen. Produce a quickly sketched plan for another setting of your choice. It could be a room or somewhere outside.
Include the five senses in your planning:

Planning the five senses

This plan also includes use of similes, metaphor and personification. These techniques work very well together with the five senses to build up descriptions of settings.

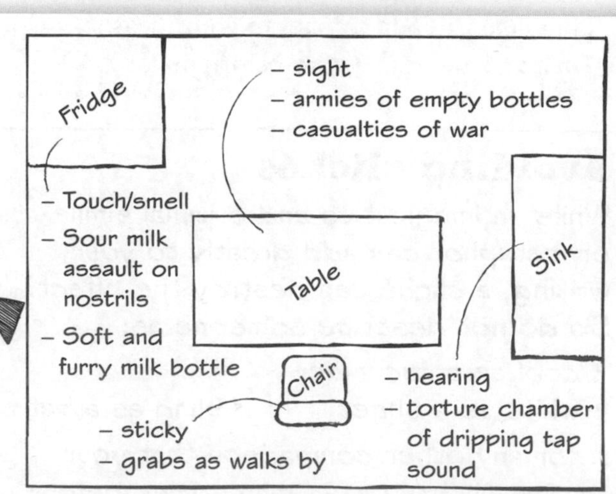

Narrative voice

In **Paper 1: Section B – Writing**, you might need to decide on the **viewpoint** of your **imaginative writing**. This is called the **narrative voice**.

See page 23 for more about narrative voice

First-person narrative

This is a narrative written in the first person ('I').

Told by an 'I' – the 'I' can be the main character or a less important character who is witnessing events.

Effective in giving a sense of closeness to the character.

Allows the story to be told in the character's distinctive voice and language.

I crashed the car when she told me. It was such an ordinary day – we were just in the car park at the shopping centre, waiting for a space to become free.

'Julie, I'm getting married.' Francesca paused for no more than one beat of my heart. 'To Michael.'

My heart banged and blood rushed through my ears as I fought for breath. With a sickening crunch the car slammed into a post, hurtling us both into our seatbelts, leaving us winded and speechless. Looking over at the passenger seat, I have to admit that I was sorry she was still breathing!

Third-person narrative

This is a narrative written in the third person. The narrator is **not** one of the characters in the story.

Characters are referred to by name or as 'he' or 'she'.

The narrator can see into any character's mind and reveal their thoughts and feelings to the reader.

An 'omniscient' (all-knowing) third-person narrator knows everything about all the characters and events.

Julie crashed the car when she heard the news. It had started as just an ordinary day for her and when the bombshell was dropped she was drumming her fingers on the steering wheel, waiting for a space to become free. Francesca said it casually, 'I'm getting married.' She paused for no more than a split second, anxious to get the news out before she lost her nerve. 'To Michael.'

The car slammed into the post with a sickening crunch, hurtling both women into their seatbelts, leaving them winded and speechless. Francesca was rigid with fear – why had she told her now? Julie was impulsive at the best of times…

Now try this

Re-read the example extracts above. Identify two advantages and two disadvantages of each narrative voice.

Remember: once you have chosen a narrative voice, stick to it throughout your answer.

Putting it into practice

For **Paper 2: Section B – Writing** you will need to show you can use language to write effectively for **different audiences and purposes**. Look at the exam-style question below and read the extracts from two students' answers.

Worked example

8 Write an article for a newspaper, exploring the idea that families with young children should not be allowed to own dogs.

You could write about:

- why you agree or disagree with the idea
- the advantages of young children owning dogs, for example, gaining a sense of responsibility, getting exercise when walking the dog
- what can go wrong when young children own dogs, for example, injuries, dogs being abandoned

… as well as any other ideas you might have.

(40 marks)

Using language in transactional writing

In each of your writing tasks you should:

- **annotate** the question to highlight the **form**, **purpose** and **audience**
- choose **language** that is appropriate for the **purpose** and **audience**
- choose **language techniques** with care and for **impact**
- **avoid** using **too many** techniques – it is more important that your writing is well structured and appropriate for the purpose and audience.

See pages 56 and 52 for reminders about writing articles and writing to argue and persuade

Sample answer

Why do parents think that letting their kids have a dog is a good idea? This week we heard about another kid being bitten in his own home by the family pet. The baby did not die, but will be scarred for life. And what will be the effect of being bitten by an animal he loved?

In my own family, our pets have caused some problems for us all…

✓ Rhetorical questions set out the point at the start and keep the reader engaged.

✗ Language too informal for form, audience and purpose.

✓ Use of evidence to support point.

✗ Unimaginative vocabulary means the writing is less persuasive.

In this sample answer, emotive words and phrases are used to shock the reader, which strengthens the writing.

Improved sample answer

Why do parents feel children's lives will be enhanced by dog ownership? For all of the upsides – and I appreciate that dogs can become a real part of the family – attacks by man's best friend have increased by 40% in the last year alone.

Yet again this week, we heard about another toddler being savaged in his own home by the family pet. Luckily, the baby did not die, but he will carry the scars for the rest of his life. And what about the consequences of being brutally mauled by a beloved and trusted member of the family?

Thankfully, my own family has not suffered to that extreme degree.

✓ Rhetorical question, with the appropriately formal language 'children', indicates the article will be serious and factual.

✓ Statistics supply evidence in the opening paragraph to create trustworthy tone.

✓ A wide range of (correctly spelled) ambitious vocabulary is used for emotive effect.

Turn to pages 91–93 for more about spelling

Now try this

Finish the third paragraph of the 'Improved sample answer' opposite, then complete the article. Remember to include a counter-argument and use adverbials to link your key points and paragraphs.

Putting it into practice

For **Paper 1: Section B – Writing** you will need to show you can use language effectively in **imaginative writing**. Look at the exam-style question below and then read the extracts from two students' answers.

Worked example

5 Write about a time when you, or someone you know, made a mistake.

You response could be real or imagined.

(40 marks)

Language choice

In each of your writing tasks you should:

- ✓ choose language appropriate to your audience
- ✓ make ambitious and effective vocabulary choices to engage your reader
- ✓ use a range of language techniques.

Sample answer

The worst mistake I ever made was jumping out of a tree. I was down the park with my friends and they dared me to climb this really tall tree. I was about eight. So I climbed up the tree. I got about a metre up and it felt like I was nearly at the sky. I looked down and realised I hadn't got very far and they were all laughing and shouting and encouraging me to go higher. So I carried on climbing. I went up another metre or so. By now I was really scared.

✗ Opening unimaginative and does not create a narrative tone.

✗ Language choice too informal and unimaginative.

✗ Limited description, and unambitious vocabulary choice.

✓ Effective use of figurative language.

Note that, although there is some limited (but effective) language choice here, there are also missed opportunities to use really effective language (as you can see in the final sentence).

Improved sample answer

My aunt had come to stay. She was a stern, grey-faced woman with eyes that could turn you to stone. When she entered a room, an arctic cold crept through the air, freezing you instantly into silence. The only thing that would make my aunt crack her face and bring out a smile was cake. She loved it. Cream cake, chocolate cake, fruit cake, any cake would bring a rosy glow to her cheeks and her long, sharpened teeth out from between her grey lips. And that was where the trouble started.

✓ Engaging vocabulary choice.

✓ Effective use of language devices:

- metaphor
- personification
- list.

Notice how this language choice shows humour as well as being effective.

Now try this

Write the first two paragraphs of your answer to the **Paper 1** exam-style question above.

Remember to choose and use:

- language appropriate to your audience
- language for effect
- a range of ambitious vocabulary and language features.

Sentence variety 1

Using a range of **different sentence types** in your **transactional** and **imaginative writing** can help you convey your ideas clearly and effectively and keep your readers engaged.

Engaging the reader

Writing for young children uses a limited range of sentence types:

Penny went out of the house.
It was raining.
Soon she was soaked.
Penny turned around and went home again.

Effective writing for adults uses a variety of sentence types to hold the reader's interest.

Sentence types

These are the basic types of sentence:

- single-clause
- multi-clause
- minor.

To remind yourself which is which, look back at page 28. You will probably want to use all of these types of sentence in your writing.

Multi-clause sentences

Multi-clause sentences can help you to keep your readers engaged with your ideas. These are the main types.

1 Sentences using a subordinate clause

- This is additional information that is added to the main clause using conjunctions such as: because, although, after, if, since.
- The subordinate clause is dependent on the main clause because it doesn't make complete sense without it.

Subordinate clause — Main clause

Although I was tired, I finished painting the walls.

You can often swap the main and subordinate clauses without changing the meaning of the sentence.

2 Sentences using a coordinate clause

If neither clause is dependent on the other, then the clauses are coordinate. Coordinate clauses use conjunctions such as: and, but, or.

Main clause — These clauses are an equal pair.

I checked that the windows were shut and I locked the front door.

3 Sentences using a relative clause

This is where additional information is introduced using a **relative pronoun**, such as: that, where, which, whose, who.

Main clause — Relative clause, separated from the main clause with commas

The neighbour, who I've never liked, waved as I walked down the front path.

Now try this

Write the opening paragraph of a response to this **Paper 1** exam-style question:

> **5** Write about a time when you, or someone you know, moved house.
> Your response could be real or imagined.
> **(40 marks)**

Aim to use at least one of:

- a single-clause sentence
- a multi-clause sentence (subordinate clause)
- a multi-clause sentence (coordinate clause)
- a multi-clause sentence (relative clause)
- a minor sentence.

Sentence variety 2

Thinking about the **first word** of your sentences can help you **add interest** to your **transactional writing** and **imaginative writing**.

First words

Developing writers often start their sentences in similar ways. Try to start your sentences in different ways to engage your reader. You can start with any of these.

Type of word	Examples
A pronoun I, you, he, she, it, we, they, my, your	I turned and started.
An article a, an, the	The glass had disappeared.
A preposition above, behind, between, near, with, etc.	Above me, I heard footsteps.
An -ing word (or present participle) running, hurrying, crawling, smiling, etc.	Edging silently to the door, I went to the stairs and listened.
An adjective slow, quiet, huge, violent, etc.	Sharp, prickling pains crept from my fingertips to my hair.
An adverb alarmingly, painfully, happily, etc.	Gingerly, I put my foot on the first stair.
A conjunction (subordinate clause + main clause) if, although, because, when, while, etc.	Although I knew I was in an empty house, I could not help thinking that I was not alone.

Now try this

Write the first **ten** sentences for this **Paper 1** exam-style question:

5 Write about when you, or someone you know, started school. Your response could be real or imagined.

(40 marks)

Getting it right

Make your writing more engaging by:

- using all seven different types of sentence opener
- using a variety of sentence types.

Sentences for different effects

Structuring your sentences in different ways can achieve different effects. For example, you can vary your sentence structure in a piece of **transactional writing** to emphasise an argument, or in your **imaginative writing** to achieve a particular mood.

Longer sentences

Use longer, **multi-clause sentences** to deliver more information sharply and concisely. You can add information using one or more subordinate clauses, as the example opposite shows.

Beware: if you overload a sentence with too much information, spread over a number of subordinate clauses, you could lose your reader's attention.

Main clause — Relative clause

The house, which I had never visited before, seemed strangely familiar.

Notice how the clauses have been separated with commas.

The long and the short

Short, punchy, **single-clause** sentences can be particularly effective: they add impact to an argument, and surprise or tension to a description. Look at the contrast opposite.

Short, single-clause sentences are particularly effective when they follow a longer multi-clause sentence.

Long sentence to contrast with a short sentence to surprise.

I wandered, marvelling in the summer sunshine, through Copenhagen's bustling streets, along the canals and over the bridges, past the vibrant colours and crowded cafes of the old port of Nyhavn, before winding back through the less-trodden back streets to my favourite bakery for a coffee and a cinnamon roll. It was Scandinavian heaven!

In order of importance

You can structure your sentences for emphasis. Important information is usually placed at the end of a sentence.

Arrange your sentences so that the point you want to emphasise comes at the end.

- This sentence gives more emphasis to the revision than the exams because it comes at the end of the sentence:

The final insult is that the dreaded exams come after all that revision.

- This sentence emphasises the dreaded exams, giving the sentence more impact:

The final insult is that after all that revision come the dreaded exams.

Now try this

8 Write a speech for a Year 11 Assembly in which you give your views on the importance of winning.

In your speech you could:

- state what type of things are worth winning and why, for example, sporting events, board games, school competitions
- describe the advantages of wanting to be the best at everything you do
- explain why winning is not always important

… as well as including any other ideas you might have.

(40 marks)

Write **one** or **two** paragraphs in response to the **Paper 2** exam-style question.

Aim to include:

- a long sentence followed by a short sentence
- a sentence structured to leave the important information until the end.

Putting it into practice

For **both papers** you will need to show that you can vary your sentences for effect. Look at the **Paper 2** exam-style question below and read the extracts from two students' answers.

Worked example

9 Write an article for a newspaper, exploring why people feel it is important to follow fashion and look good.

You could write about:

- what type of fashionable objects people buy, for example, clothes, mobile phones, shoes
- why people feel that fashion is so important
- the problems that following fashion can cause

... as well as any other ideas you might have.

(40 marks)

Sentence variety

In each of the writing tasks you should:

- ✓ use a range of sentence structures
- ✓ start your sentences in different ways
- ✓ structure your sentences for effect.

Sample answer

Fashion is important because people judge you on how you look, even though you shouldn't it's difficult not to. Fashion can also be fun because shopping and choosing clothes and seeing what your friends are wearing are really enjoyable. Fashion is also something to talk about and do with your friends because if all your friends are in fashion and like the same fashion then you can swap clothes and tell them how they look.

Notice that:

- each sentence starts in the same way
- each sentence follows the same structure
- sentences are all long, using multiple clauses.

To improve your answer you should add variety.

✗ Vocabulary is frequently repeated.

✗ A limited range of adverbials creates repetitive vocabulary and sentence structure.

Improved sample answer

We all judge a book by its cover. We don't mean to but we do. But should we? Even if we don't want to judge others, we expect others to judge us. We primp, preen and polish ourselves for hours, preparing ourselves to be seen by the world. How disappointing would it be if, after all that effort, no one bothered to look and make the right judgement? The truth is that, no matter how much we might not want appearances to matter, they do. They matter very much.

Notice how this answer starts with:

- two short sentences to create an emphatic opening
- a rhetorical question to engage the reader
- a neatly structured sentence.

✓ A second rhetorical question further engages the reader.

✓ Long sentence, followed by powerful short sentence, further emphasised with repetition.

Now try this

Write the **first two** paragraphs of your own answer to **Paper 2** exam-style question 9 above.

Remember to:

- use a range of sentence types and lengths
- start sentences in a variety of ways
- structure sentences for effect.

Ending a sentence

In **both papers** your writing will be marked for the quality of your **punctuation**. Make sure you start each sentence with a **capital letter**. End each sentence with a **full stop, an exclamation mark** or **a question mark**.

Check your full stops

Most students know that a sentence should start with a capital letter and end with a full stop. However, mistakes are often made. The most common error is using a comma to join two sentences instead of a full stop to separate them. This is called a **comma splice.**

Avoiding the comma splice

When you want to tell the reader two pieces of information you can do two things.

Separate them with a full stop:

The countryside is green and peaceful. It can sometimes be too quiet.

Join them with a conjunction:

The countryside is green and peaceful **but** it can sometimes be too quiet.

You **cannot** join them with a comma:

The countryside is green and peaceful, it can sometimes be too quiet.

Question marks

Always check you have actually put a question mark at the end of a question – especially if it is a rhetorical question.

Exclamation marks

Be **very** careful in your use of exclamation marks. Follow these golden rules:

- Only use an exclamation mark for a real exclamation, e.g. 'Thank goodness!' he cried.
- Use them very sparingly. Don't scatter them randomly throughout your writing.
- Never use two or more exclamation marks in a row.

Now try this

Rewrite this student's answer, removing all the comma splices. Try to do this in three different ways by:

- adding conjunctions
- restructuring some of the sentences
- replacing the comma splices with full stops.

Remember that you do not use a comma to join two pieces of information in a sentence. Use a full stop to separate them, or a conjunction or a semi-colon to join them.

I was born in the countryside, I grew up surrounded by the sounds and smells of the natural world, when I was ten we moved to the city; it was a confusing, fast-paced, deafening environment that I found hard to love. It was such a big change, it came as quite a shock to my system, worst of all I had to leave all my friends behind and try to make new ones in this strange, unfamiliar place. I was lonely, convinced I would never feel at home, before a year had passed I had the best friend anyone could wish for.

Commas

It is very important that you feel confident using **commas**, as you will need to use them to create **effective multi-clause sentences** and **lists**.

Also see page 28 for a reminder about sentence types

Commas and subordinate clauses

In a multi-clause sentence, the main clause and the subordinate clause can usually be swapped around without changing the meaning of the sentence:

I meet new people (main clause) wherever I go. (subordinate clause)

If you begin a multi-clause sentence with the main clause, there is no need for a comma to separate the clauses.

Wherever I go, (subordinate clause) I meet new people. (main clause)

If you begin a multi-clause sentence with the subordinate clause, use a comma to separate it from the main clause.

Commas and relative clauses

You can add a relative clause to a sentence, giving additional information linked with one of these relative pronouns:

- that
- whose
- where
- who
- which
- when.

You should always separate the relative clause from the main clause with commas.

Main clause — Relative clause

The house, which I had never visited before, seemed strangely familiar.

Notice how the clauses have been separated with commas.

Commas in a list

If you are writing a list, add a comma after each word or phrase – apart from the words or phrases that are linked using 'and'.

- Use commas in lists of adjectives:

He was tall, smartly dressed and elegant.

Comma here to separate two items in a list.

No comma here because they are linked with 'and'.

- Use commas in lists of phrases:

There was mud on the floor, mud on the walls, mud on the windows and mud on the ceiling.

Now try this

Look at the **Paper 1** exam-style question. Write **three** to **five** sentences, using commas correctly to separate:

- items in a list
- a main and subordinate clause
- a main and relative clause.

End your sentences correctly. Avoid using a **comma splice**.

5 Write about a time when you, or someone you know, went on a school trip.
Your response could be real or imagined.
(40 marks)

Apostrophes and speech punctuation

Missing or incorrect **apostrophes** and **speech punctuation** are common errors. You may wish to use dialogue in **both papers**, so make sure you know how to avoid mistakes.

Apostrophes in contractions

When two words are shortened or abbreviated, some letters are missed out or omitted. You should use an apostrophe to show where these letters are missing:

cannot → **can't**
do not → **don't**
I will → **I'll**
let us → **let's**

Abbreviations such as **don't** and **can't** are more informal than the full, unabbreviated versions. Think about your audience when deciding which to use.

Apostrophes of possession

Apostrophes can be used to show that someone or something belongs to someone or something else.

- The boy's hands ...
- Betty's sister ...
- The dog's collar ...
- The school's head teacher ...

Note that if the word to which you are adding the apostrophe ends in s you can just add the apostrophe after the s:

The teachers' voices

Mrs Roberts' book

Note that this is a plural: there is more than one teacher.

You can also, when a name ends in s, add an apostrophe and another s.

Mrs Roberts's book

Speech punctuation

- Use speech marks to enclose the words that are spoken.
- Start the speech with a capital letter.
- There is always a punctuation mark just before the closing speech marks.
- Use a comma if you are adding who is speaking ...
- ... followed by a lower case letter immediately after the closing speech marks.
- Use a full stop if you are not adding who is speaking.

'Mum, can I have some sweets?' begged Aran.

'It's nearly dinner time,' his mother replied.

'Mum, I want some sweets.'

'I've just told you,' said his mother patiently.

Avoid too much dialogue in imaginative writing. Focus on full paragraphs of prose to show you understand sentence structures.

Now try this

There are **13** punctuation errors in this student's writing. Copy and correct it.

'theres nothing I can do said Garys dad.
'are you sure,' Replied Gary.
'idont know what you mean.' Said his dad.
'i think you do'

Colons, semi-colons, dashes, brackets and ellipses

Punctuation can help you develop your ideas and express yourself clearly.

Semi-colons

You can **link two connected ideas** with a semi-colon instead of a conjunction.

For example, you could write:

> Education is a privilege and it should be treasured.

Or you could write:

> Education is a privilege; it should be treasured.

Dashes and brackets

These can be used to **add** extra, but not entirely necessary, information to a sentence. Before using brackets or dashes, ask yourself: Is this important information? Or would my writing be better without it?

Dashes can be used in **pairs** to add information mid-sentence:

> Several years ago – though I can't remember exactly when – my sister moved to Scotland.

Single dashes can be used at the end of a sentence, to suggest a pause before an afterthought:

> I'm sure there was a reason – but no one ever told me what it was.

Brackets must be used in **pairs**:

> The house (which my mother hated) was near the sea.

Colons

Use a colon to **introduce an example**:

> Students have two choices: work hard or fail.

Or to **introduce a list**:

> You will need: a pen, a pencil, a ruler and an eraser.

Or to **introduce an explanation**:

> English is my favourite subject: I love imaginative writing.

Ellipses

You can use an ellipsis in **dialogue** to suggest a **dramatic pause** or to show someone falling into **silence**:

> 'I don't know where I...'
> He looked mystified.

> 'And the winner is...'

Using an ellipsis to suggest tension in descriptive writing can seem clichéd. Instead, create tension through your choice of language and sentence structure:

> He opened the door and realised to his horror that the room was completely empty...

> He opened the door. The room was completely empty.

Now try this

Answer the following questions using the information on this page.

1 What punctuation could you use to introduce an explanation?
2 What could you use instead of a conjunction to link two connected ideas?
3 When might you use a pair of dashes?

Putting it into practice

For **both papers** you will need to show you can use a range of punctuation accurately. Look at the **Paper 2** exam-style question below and read the extracts from two students' answers.

Worked example

8 Enter a competition your school magazine is running by writing an article with the title 'I couldn't live without …'.
In your article you could:
- write about anything that is important to you, for example, a hobby, a pet, a person or an item
- describe your important thing or person
- explain why the thing or person is important to you

… as well as including any other ideas you might have.

(40 marks)

Punctuation

In each of the writing tasks you need to show you can:

 punctuate accurately

 use a full range of punctuation

 use punctuation effectively to express yourself clearly.

Sample answer

I could'nt live without football, its something I've always loved. I love playing it and watching it whether its a few friends having a kickabout at lunchtime or an FA Cup final on the telly. There are lots of reasons it means so much to me. One is that my dad loves football so its something we have in common. He does'nt play football but we can spend hours talking about it, who scored, who didnt score who should be playing and who should be dropped.

✗ Incorrectly placed apostrophes.

✗ Comma splice. This should either be a semi-colon or a full stop followed by a new sentence.

✗ Missing apostrophe.

✗ Missed opportunity for a colon to introduce a list.

✗ Missing comma separating items in a list.

Note that the use of full stops in the first answer is **generally** accurate.

Improved sample answer

The only thing which I cannot imagine ever being without is my dog. She doesn't bark, she doesn't growl, she doesn't jump up; she's perfect in every way. Just the sight of her floppy ears, her wagging tail and her shiny black eyes can put a smile on my face. I remember when I got her: it was my ninth birthday, a day I will always remember. I opened all my presents – none of which I can remember now – and my mum said she had one more surprise for me. She brought in a small cardboard box.

The full stops in the improved answer are **completely** accurate.

✓ Correct use of apostrophe.

✓ Commas, semi-colons and colons are all used accurately. Notice how the commas separate items in a list, the colon is used to introduce an explanation, and the semi-colon acts like a full stop.

Dashes like these are used to add additional information.

Now try this

Write the first paragraph of your answer to the above exam-style question. Aim to use a range of punctuation accurately, including commas, apostrophes, colons and semi-colons.

Always remember to check your punctuation – especially full stops – for accuracy.

Common spelling errors 1

For **both papers** you will need to show you can spell correctly. There are some spelling mistakes that occur again and again in students' exam responses. Learn how to avoid making them.

Would have, could have, should have

Students often use **would of** or **should of** or **could of** when they should use **would have**, **should have**, or **could have**. For example:

Global warming could of been prevented. We should of started thinking more carefully about the environment long ago.

This is what should have been written:
could **have** ✓ should **have** ✓

Our, are

Students often confuse *our* and *are*:

- **our** means *belonging to us*
- **are** is from the verb *to be*.

We should always look after are bodies. They our precious.

This is what should have been written:
our bodies ✓ **are** precious ✓

There, their, they're

Make sure you learn these spellings:

- **their** means belonging to **them**
- **there** is used to describe the position of something **(It's over there)** and in the phrases **There is** or **There are**
- **they're** is an abbreviation of **they are**.

Their were three people at the table, all eating there dinner.

~~Their~~ There were three people at the table, all eating ~~there~~ their dinner.

Affect, effect

One of these is a verb, and the other a noun:
affect is a verb
effect is usually used as a noun.
So, for example, you may have been **affected** by a problem. But the problem had an **effect** on you. If the word has got **an** or **the** in front of it, it's a noun, so it's spelt **effect**.

Remember: don't be afraid to use an effective word because you're not sure about the spelling.

-ly or -ley?

When you add -ly to a word, make sure you don't swap the 'l' and the 'e':

definite + ly = definitely

bravley ✗ bravely ✓
safley ✗ safely ✓
rudley ✗ rudely ✓

There are **very few** words which end in -ley. Learn these examples: alley, medley, trolley, valley.

Its or it's?

It's is an abbreviation of **it is**. **Its** means belonging to **it**.

✗ Its the end of it's life.

✓ ~~Its~~ It's the end of ~~it's~~ its life.

Now try this

Look back at the last five pieces of writing you have completed. Have you made any of these common spelling errors? If so, correct them.

Had a look ☐ Nearly there ☐ Nailed it! ☐

Common spelling errors 2

Your and you're

Learn the difference between these two words:

- **your** means **belonging to you**
- **you're** is an abbreviation of **you are.**

✗ Your having the time of you're life.

✓ ~~Your~~ You're having the time of ~~you're~~ your life.

Remember: **A lot** is two words. **Alot of people love chocolate** is wrong, but **A lot of people love chocolate** is correct.

We're, wear, were and where

Make sure you are familiar with each of these:

- **we're** is an abbreviation of **we are**
- **wear** is a verb referring to clothing – e.g. **What are you wearing tonight?**
- **were** is the past tense of are – e.g. **they are, they were**
- **where** is a question word referring to place – e.g. **Where are we going?**

✗ Wear we're you? Were leaving now.

~~Wear we're~~ Where were you? ~~Were~~ We're leaving now.

Two, too, to

Getting these words wrong is quite a common error:

- **to** indicates place, direction or position – e.g. **I went to Spain.**
- **too** means **also** or an **excessive amount** – e.g. **I went too far.**
- **two** is a number.

✗ It's to difficult to get too the highest level.

✓ It's ~~to~~ too difficult to get ~~too~~ to the highest level.

Of, off

The easiest way to remember the difference is by listening to the sound of the word you want to use:

- **of** is pronounced ov
- **off** rhymes with cough.

✗ He jumped of the top off the wall.

✓ He jumped ~~of~~ off the top ~~off~~ of the wall.

Past, passed

Aim to get these two right:

- **passed** is the past tense of the verb to pass – e.g. **He passed all his GCSEs.**
- **past** refers to time that has gone by, or *position* – e.g. **That's all in the past; He ran past the school.**

✗ She past out at ten passed six.

✓ She ~~past~~ passed out at ten ~~passed~~ past six.

Who's and whose

Whose is a question word referring to belonging, e.g. **Whose book is this?**

Who's is an abbreviation of **who is.**

✗ Whose wearing who's coat?

✓ ~~Whose~~ Who's wearing ~~who's~~ whose coat?

Now try this

There are **nine** spelling errors in this student's writing. Copy and correct it.

I saw Annabel walk passed wearing you're shoes. She was carrying you're bag to. I don't know who's coat she had on but it had too stripes across the back. She stopped and took it of. I don't know were she was going or what she was up two. It was very strange.

Commons spelling errors 3

Some of the most frequently misspelt words are listed below. Make sure you learn how to spell them correctly.

amusement
argument

Notice the 'e' here but not here.

opportunity
disappoint
embarrassing
beginning
occasionally
difficult
disappear
possession
recommend

Check which letters are **doubled** and which are not.

privilege
definitely
separately
conscious
conscience
experience
independence

Look closely at the vowels – 'e', 'i' or 'a'.

business — Silent 'i' in the middle.

believe weird — 'ei' or 'ie'?

rhythm — Two 'h's, but no vowels.

decision — Get the 'c' and the 's' round the right way.

grateful — Not greatful; **grate**ful = to show **grat**itude.

Learning correct spellings

Find a hidden word. Look for words hidden within the word you are learning. For example, **separate** becomes much easier to remember when you notice that there's a rat in the middle of it:

sep **a rat** e

Say what you see. Say the word aloud, breaking it up into syllables and pronouncing them as they are written. For example, read these syllables aloud:

def / in / ite / ly

Now try this

Test yourself on these spellings. Learn any that you get wrong, then you could ask a friend or family member to re-test you.

Had a look ☐ Nearly there ☐ Nailed it! ☐

Proofreading

For **both papers** it is essential that you leave time at the end of the exam to **check your work**. It could make all the difference.

What kinds of mistakes do you make?

Here's a list of common errors:

- spelling mistakes
- missing or incorrect punctuation
- grammatical errors such as misused, repeated or missing words
- using the wrong tense, or changing tense, for instance, 'he rushed towards the door, *puts* his key in the lock and shouted.'

Most people make **all three** kinds of mistakes, especially when they are writing in a hurry.

Ideally, you should check your work through three times:

- once for spelling
- once for punctuation
- once to check it makes clear sense, with no misused, repeated or missing words.

You **will** have made mistakes. Aim to find **five or more** in each of your answers.

Checking for sense: tips

1. When you are checking for sense, try to read 'aloud inside your head' imagining you can hear your voice.
2. Remember to leave time to check your work at the end of the exam. If you check each answer as soon as you've finished writing it, you'll see what you **think** you wrote, not what you **actually** wrote.
3. If you come across a sentence that is clumsy, doesn't make sense, or both... cross it out and try expressing it in a different way.

Alarm bells

Train your proofreading brain to ring an alarm bell whenever you come across their, there, its, it's or any one of the common spelling errors that everyone makes. When the alarm rings, **stop!** Double check that you've used the correct spelling.

How to check your spelling

If you know you've spelt a word incorrectly, but you're not sure of the correct spelling, try it three or four different ways in the margin. Pick the one that looks right:

seperatly	separetly
separately ✓	separatley

Reading your work backwards – from bottom to top, right to left – stops you thinking about the meaning of your writing and makes you focus on spelling.

Putting it right

Accurate writing achieves higher marks than neat writing. So, if you find a mistake – whether it's a word, a sentence, or a whole paragraph – **cross it out**. Put **one neat line** through the mistake and add your correction by:

- using one of these ⁄ ~~to make a mistake~~ (to guide the reader)
- or by using an asterisk.*

* To tell the reader to read this bit next.

If you forget to start a new paragraph, use // to mark where one paragraph ends and the next one begins.

Now try this

Look over five pieces of writing you have produced recently. How many mistakes can you find?

Putting it into practice

For **both papers**, your writing needs to be as **accurate** as possible. You need to check your work for **errors** in **spelling, punctuation** and **grammar**. Look at the **Paper 2** exam-style question below and read the extracts from two students' answers.

Worked example

9 Write an article for a newspaper exploring the idea that every teenager should have a part-time job.
You could write about:
- the types of jobs that are available to teenagers
- why it is a good idea for teenagers to have a part-time job
- the disadvantages of teenagers working

… as well as any other ideas you might have.

(40 marks)

Proofreading

For all your writing tasks you should:

- ✓ spend about 3–5 minutes carefully checking your work
- ✓ correct any spelling errors
- ✓ correct any punctuation errors
- ✓ ensure your writing makes clear sense and is legible.

Finding and changing errors could really improve your answer.

Sample answer

Everyone says GCSEs have got easyer but they dont realise how difficult they are and how how much work we have to do at school. There just isn't time to do all the school work and have a part-time job, we need some to rest and and enjoy ourselves. On an avarage day I go to school for six hours, get home and do an hour or two of homework. I could go out to work in the evenings but Id get home late and be realy tired at school the next day which would make it realy dificult to concentrate at school the next day.

Make sure you spend some time checking your answers. The second sentence:
- is clumsily written
- has errors
- is not clear in its meaning.

✗ Spelling errors

✗ Punctuation errors

Improved sample answer

Working for my money has certainly taught me its value. For example, when I was younger and wanted to buy something, I had to pester my mum.* Now, because I've e^a^rned my money, ~~I can buy what I want. Because of that I always make sure I know I want what I'm buying.~~ I make very sure I'm not wasting my money on something I ~~dont~~ → don't really need.

* Usually, once I'd got it, I would realise that I didn't really want it any more.

✓ Spelling and punctuation errors both corrected.

✓ The additional explanation effectively reinforces the argument.

It's fine to cross out clumsy writing and add in something that is easier to read and understand.

Now try this

Look back at a piece of writing you have completed recently. Check it **three** times, looking for:
- sentences that are clumsily written or unclear
- missing or repeated words
- spelling mistakes
- punctuation errors.

Aim to find at least **five** mistakes and correct them.

TEXTS

Cut along the dotted lines and staple the texts together to make your own handy anthology. Make sure you keep it safe with your Revision Guide.

TEXT 1

This is an extract from the opening chapter of a novel. Marseilles is a city on the southern coast of France

***Little Dorrit*: Charles Dickens**

Blinds, shutters, curtains, awnings, were all closed and drawn to keep out the stare. Grant it but a chink or keyhole, and it shot in like a white-hot arrow. The churches were the freest from it. To come out of the twilight of pillars and arches – dreamily dotted with winking lamps, dreamily peopled with ugly old shadows piously[1] dozing, spitting, and begging – was to plunge into a fiery river, and swim for life to the nearest strip of shade. So, with people lounging and lying wherever shade was, with but little hum of tongues or barking of dogs, with occasional jangling of discordant[2] church bells and rattling of vicious drums, Marseilles, a fact to be strongly smelt and tasted, lay broiling in the sun one day.

In Marseilles that day there was a villainous prison. In one of its chambers, so repulsive a place that even the obtrusive[3] stare blinked at it, and left it to such refuse of reflected light as it could find for itself, were two men. Besides the two men, a notched and disfigured bench, immovable from the wall, with a draught-board rudely hacked upon it with a knife, a set of draughts, made of old buttons and soup bones, a set of dominoes, two mats, and two or three wine bottles. That was all the chamber held, exclusive of rats and other unseen vermin, in addition to the seen vermin, the two men.

It received such light as it got through a grating of iron bars fashioned like a pretty large window, by means of which it could be always inspected from the gloomy staircase on which the grating gave. There was a broad strong ledge of stone to this grating where the bottom of it was let into the masonry[4], three or four feet above the ground. Upon it, one of the two men lolled, half sitting and half lying, with his knees drawn up, and his feet and shoulders planted against the opposite sides of the aperture[5]. The bars were wide enough apart to admit of his thrusting his arm through to the elbow; and so he held on negligently, for his greater ease.

A prison taint[6] was on everything there. The imprisoned air, the imprisoned light, the imprisoned damps, the imprisoned men, were all deteriorated by confinement. As the captive men were faded and haggard, so the iron was rusty, the stone was slimy, the wood was rotten, the air was faint, the light was dim. Like a well, like a vault, like a tomb, the prison had no knowledge of the brightness outside, and would have kept its polluted atmosphere intact in one of the spice islands of the Indian ocean.

The man who lay on the ledge of the grating was even chilled. He jerked his great cloak more heavily upon him by an impatient movement of one shoulder, and growled, 'To the devil with this Brigand[7] of a Sun that never shines in here!'

He was waiting to be fed, looking sideways through the bars that he might see the further down the stairs, with much of the expression of a wild beast in similar expectation. But his eyes, too close together, were not so nobly set in his head as those of the king of beasts are in his, and they were sharp rather than bright – pointed weapons with little surface to betray them. They had no depth or change; they glittered, and they opened and shut. So far, and waiving their use to himself, a clockmaker could have made a better pair. He had a hook nose, handsome after its kind, but too high between the eyes by probably just as much as his eyes were too near to one another. For the rest, he was large and tall in frame, had thin lips, where his thick moustache showed them at all, and a quantity of dry hair, of no definable colour, in its shaggy state, but shot with[8] red. The hand with which he held the grating (seamed all over the back with ugly scratches newly healed), was unusually small and plump; would have been unusually white but for the prison grime.

The other man was lying on the stone floor, covered with a coarse brown coat.

'Get up, pig!' growled the first. 'Don't sleep when I am hungry.'

'It's all one, master,' said the pig, in a submissive manner, and not without cheerfulness; 'I can wake when I will, I can sleep when I will. It's all the same.'

As he said it, he rose, shook himself, scratched himself, tied his brown coat loosely round his neck by the sleeves (he had previously used it as a coverlet), and sat down upon the pavement yawning, with his back against the wall opposite to the grating.

'Say what the hour is,' grumbled the first man.

'The mid-day bells will ring – in forty minutes.' When he made the little pause, he had looked round the prison-room, as if for certain information.

1: *piously* – religiously
2: *discordant* – not in tune
3: *obtrusive* – pushy and unwelcome
4: *masonry* – stonework
5: *aperture* – opening
6: *taint* – smell or contamination
7: *Brigand* – robber
8: *shot with* – mixed with

Cut along the dotted lines and staple the texts together to make your own handy anthology. Make sure you keep it safe with your Revision Guide.

TEXT 2

This is an extract from a short story. The narrator, Samuel Lowgood, and his colleague, Christopher Weldon, are rivals for the affections of Lucy Malden.

***Samuel Lowgood's Revenge:* Mary E. Braddon**

I, too, was an orphan; but I was doubly an orphan. My father and mother had both died in my infancy. I had been reared in a workhouse, had picked up chance waifs and strays of education from the hardest masters, and had been drafted, at the age of ten, into the offices of Tyndale and Tyndale. Errand boy, light porter, office drudge, junior clerk – one by one I had mounted the rounds in this troublesome ladder, which for me could only be begun from the very bottom; and at the age of twenty-one I found myself – where? In a business character, I was on a level with Christopher Weldon, the son of a gentleman. How often I, the pauper orphan of a bankrupt corn-chandler[1], had to hear this phrase – the son of a gentleman! In a business character, I say, I, Samuel Lowgood, who had worked and slaved and drudged, had been snubbed, throughout eleven long weary years – and in spite of all had become a clever accountant and a thorough arithmetician – was in the same rank as Christopher Weldon, who had been in the office exactly four weeks, just to see, as his mother said, whether it would suit him.

He was about as much good in the counting-house as a wax doll would have been, and, like a wax doll, he looked very pretty; but Messrs Tyndale and Tyndale had known his father; and Tyndale senior knew his uncle, and Tyndale junior was acquainted with his first cousin, who lived at the court-end of London; so he was taken at once into the office as junior clerk, with every chance, as one of the seniors told me confidentially, of rising much higher, if he took care of himself.

He knew about as much arithmetic as a baby; but he was very clever with his pen in sketching pretty girls with powdered heads, flowing sacques[2], and pannier-hoops[3]; so he found plenty of amusement in doing this and reading Mr Henry Fielding's novels behind the ledger; and the head clerks left him to himself, and snubbed me for not doing his work as well as my own.

I hated him. I hated his foppish[4] ways and his haughty manners; I hated his handsome boyish face, with its frame of golden hair, and its blue, beaming, hopeful eyes; I hated him for the sword which swung across the stiff skirts of his brocaded[5] coat, for the money which he jingled in his waistcoat pockets, for the two watches which he wore on high days and holidays, for his merry laugh, for his melodious voice, for his graceful walk, for his tall, slender figure, for his jovial, winning ways, which won everybody else's friendship. I hated him for all these; but, most of all, I hated him for his influence over Lucy Malden.

1: *corn-chandler* – dealer in corn
2: *sacques* – dresses
3: *pannier-hoops* – frames worn under dresses to make them fall in a dome-like shape
4: *foppish* – vain
5: *brocaded* – patterned with gold and silver thread

TEXTS

Cut along the dotted lines and staple the texts together to make your own handy anthology. Make sure you keep it safe with your Revision Guide.

TEXT 3

This is an extract from a novel. Tom and Becky are children who have wandered away from a picnic and got lost in a cave.

***The Adventures of Tom Sawyer*: Mark Twain**

"Do you remember this?" said he.

Becky almost smiled.

"It's our wedding-cake, Tom."

"Yes—I wish it was as big as a barrel, for it's all we've got."

"I saved it from the picnic for us to dream on, Tom, the way grownup people do with wedding-cake—but it'll be our—"

She dropped the sentence where it was. Tom divided the cake and Becky ate with good appetite, while Tom nibbled at his moiety[1]. There was abundance of cold water to finish the feast with. By-and-by Becky suggested that they move on again. Tom was silent a moment. Then he said:

"Becky, can you bear it if I tell you something?"

Becky's face paled, but she thought she could.

"Well, then, Becky, we must stay here, where there's water to drink. That little piece is our last candle!"

Becky gave loose to tears and wailings. Tom did what he could to comfort her, but with little effect. At length Becky said:

"Tom!"

"Well, Becky?"

"They'll miss us and hunt for us!"

"Yes, they will! Certainly they will!"

"Maybe they're hunting for us now, Tom."

"Why, I reckon maybe they are. I hope they are."

"When would they miss us, Tom?"

"When they get back to the boat, I reckon."

"Tom, it might be dark then—would they notice we hadn't come?"

"I don't know. But anyway, your mother would miss you as soon as they got home."

A frightened look in Becky's face brought Tom to his senses and he saw that he had made a blunder. Becky was not to have gone home that night! The children became silent and thoughtful. In a moment a new burst of grief from Becky showed Tom that the thing in his mind had struck hers also—that the Sabbath morning might be half spent before Mrs. Thatcher discovered that Becky was not at Mrs. Harper's.

The children fastened their eyes upon their bit of candle and watched it melt slowly and pitilessly away; saw the half inch of wick stand alone at last; saw the feeble flame rise and fall, climb the thin column of smoke, linger at its top a moment, and then—the horror of utter darkness reigned!

How long afterward it was that Becky came to a slow consciousness that she was crying in Tom's arms, neither could tell. All that they knew was, that after what seemed a mighty stretch of time, both awoke out of a dead stupor of sleep and resumed their miseries once more. Tom said it might be Sunday, now—maybe Monday. He tried to get Becky to talk, but her sorrows were too oppressive, all her hopes were gone. Tom said that they must have been missed long ago, and no doubt the search was going on. He would shout and maybe some one would come. He tried it; but in the darkness the distant echoes sounded so hideously that he tried it no more.

The hours wasted away, and hunger came to torment the captives again. A portion of Tom's half of the cake was left; they divided and ate it. But they seemed hungrier than before. The poor morsel of food only whetted[2] desire.

By-and-by Tom said:

"SH! Did you hear that?"

Both held their breath and listened. There was a sound like the faintest, far-off shout. Instantly Tom answered it, and leading Becky by the hand, started groping down the corridor in its direction. Presently he listened again; again the sound was heard, and apparently a little nearer.

"It's them!" said Tom; "they're coming! Come along, Becky—we're all right now!"

The joy of the prisoners was almost overwhelming. Their speed was slow, however, because pitfalls were somewhat common, and had to be guarded against. They shortly came to one and had to stop. It might be three feet deep, it might be a hundred—there was no passing it at any rate. Tom got down on his breast and reached as far down as he could. No bottom. They must stay there and wait until the searchers came. They listened; evidently the distant shoutings were growing more distant! A moment or two more and they had gone altogether. The heart-sinking misery of it! Tom whooped until he was hoarse, but it was of no use. He talked hopefully to Becky; but an age of anxious waiting passed and no sounds came again.

The children groped their way back to the spring. The weary time dragged on; they slept again, and awoke famished and woe-stricken[3]. Tom believed it must be Tuesday by this time.

1: *moiety* – half
2: *whetted* – triggered
3: *woe-stricken* – miserable, distressed

Cut along the dotted lines and staple the texts together to make your own handy anthology. Make sure you keep it safe with your Revision Guide.

TEXT 4

This is an extract from a short story. The narrator has been sent on an errand by his father and finds himself lost in bad weather.

***The Half-Brothers:* Elizabeth Gaskell**

It looked dark and gloomy enough; but everything was so still that I thought I should have plenty of time to get home before the snow came down. Off I set at a pretty quick pace. But night came on quicker. The right path was clear enough in the day-time, although at several points two or three exactly similar diverged from the same place; but when there was a good light, the traveller was guided by the sight of distant objects,—a piece of rock,—a fall in the ground—which were quite invisible to me now. I plucked up a brave heart, however, and took what seemed to me the right road. It was wrong, nevertheless, and led me whither I knew not, but to some wild boggy moor[1] where the solitude seemed painful, intense, as if never footfall of man had come thither to break the silence. I tried to shout—with the dimmest possible hope of being heard—rather to reassure myself by the sound of my own voice; but my voice came husky and short, and yet it dismayed me; it seemed so weird and strange, in that noiseless expanse of black darkness. Suddenly the air was filled thick with dusky flakes, my face and hands were wet with snow. It cut me off from the slightest knowledge of where I was, for I lost every idea of the direction from which I had come, so that I could not even retrace my steps; it hemmed me in, thicker, thicker, with a darkness that might be felt. The boggy soil on which I stood quaked under me if I remained long in one place, and yet I dared not move far. All my youthful hardiness seemed to leave me at once. I was on the point of crying, and only very shame seemed to keep it down. To save myself from shedding tears, I shouted—terrible, wild shouts for bare life they were. I turned sick as I paused to listen; no answering sound came but the unfeeling echoes. Only the noiseless, pitiless snow kept falling thicker, thicker—faster, faster! I was growing numb and sleepy. I tried to move about, but I dared not go far, for fear of the precipices[2] which, I knew, abounded in certain places on the Fells[3]. Now and then, I stood still and shouted again; but my voice was getting choked with tears, as I thought of the desolate helpless death I was to die, and how little they at home, sitting round the warm, red, bright fire, wotted[4] what was become of me,—and how my poor father would grieve for me—it would surely kill him—it would break his heart, poor old man! Aunt Fanny too—was this to be the end of all her cares for me? I began to review my life in a strange kind of vivid dream, in which the various scenes of my few boyish years passed before me like visions. In a pang of agony, caused by such remembrance of my short life, I gathered up my strength and called out once more, a long, despairing, wailing cry, to which I had no hope of obtaining any answer, save from the echoes around, dulled as the sound might be by the thickened air. To my surprise I heard a cry—almost as long, as wild as mine—so wild that it seemed unearthly, and I almost thought it must be the voice of some of the mocking spirits of the Fells, about whom I had heard so many tales. My heart suddenly began to beat fast and loud. I could not reply for a minute or two. I nearly fancied I had lost the power of utterance.

1: *moor* – wild, open land
2: *precipices* – high, steep rock faces or cliffs
3: *Fells* – hills
4: *wotted* – knew

TEXTS

Cut along the dotted lines and staple the texts together to make your own handy anthology. Make sure you keep it safe with your Revision Guide.

TEXT 5

Frank McCourt was an Irish-American writer. In his prize-winning memoir, Angela's Ashes, *he describes the hardships of his childhood in Ireland in the 1930s and 1940s.*

***Angela's Ashes:* Frank McCourt**

There are telegram boys sitting on a bench along a wall. There are two women at a desk, one fat, one thin. The thin one says, Yes?

My name is Frank McCourt, miss, and I'm here to start work.

What kind of work would that be now?

Telegram boy, miss.

The thin one cackles, Oh, God, I thought you were here to clean the lavatories.

No, miss. My mother brought a note from the priest, Dr. Cowpar, and there's supposed to be a job.

Oh, there is, is there? And do you know what day this is?

I do, miss. 'Tis my birthday. I'm fourteen.

Isn't that grand, says the fat woman.

Today is Thursday, says the thin woman. Your job starts on Monday. Go away and wash yourself and come back then.

The telegram boys along the wall are laughing. I don't know why but I feel my face turning hot. I tell the women, Thank you, and on the way out I hear the thin one, Jesus above, Maureen, who dragged in that specimen? and they laugh along with the telegram boys.

Aunt Aggie says, Well? and I tell her I don't start till Monday. She says my clothes are a disgrace and what did I wash them in.

Carbolic soap[1].

They smell like dead pigeons and you're making a laughing stock of the whole family.

She takes me to Roche's Stores and buys me a shirt, a gansey[2], a pair of short pants, two pairs of stockings and a pair of summer shoes on sale. She gives me two shillings to have tea and a bun for my birthday. She gets on the bus to go back up O'Connell Street too fat and lazy to walk. Fat and lazy, no son of her own, and still she buys me the clothes for my new job.

I turn toward Arthur's Quay with the package of new clothes under my arm and I have to stand at the edge of the River Shannon so that the whole world won't see the tears of a man the day he's fourteen.

Monday morning I'm up early to wash my face and flatten my hair with water and spit. The Abbot sees me in my new clothes. Jaysus, he says, is it gettin' married you are? and goes back to sleep.

Mrs. O'Connell, the fat woman, says, Well, well, aren't we the height of fashion, and the thin one, Miss Barry, says, Did you rob a bank on the weekend? and there's a great laugh from the telegram boys sitting on the bench along the wall.

I'm told to sit at the end of the bench and wait for my turn to go out with telegrams. Some telegram boys in uniforms are the permanent ones who took the exam. They can stay in the post office forever if they like, take the next exam for postman and then the one for clerk that lets them work inside selling stamps and money orders behind the counter downstairs. The post office gives permanent boys big waterproof capes for the bad weather and they get two weeks holiday every year. Everyone says these are good jobs, steady and pensionable and respectable, and if you get a job like this you never have to worry again in your whole life, so you don't.

Temporary telegram boys are not allowed to stay in the job beyond the age of sixteen. There are no uniforms, no holidays, the pay is less, and if you stay out sick a day you can be fired. No excuses. There are no waterproof capes. Bring your own raincoat or dodge the raindrops.

1: *carbolic soap* – a strong, antiseptic soap for washing the body, not clothes
2: *gansey* – sweater or T-shirt

Cut along the dotted lines and staple the texts together to make your own handy anthology. Make sure you keep it safe with your Revision Guide.

TEXT 6

This is a complete piece of writing from A Stranger at My Table, *a collection of texts by women about bringing up teenagers.*

Notes from a Grandmother

There is life after teenage. Hard to believe when you're facing a screaming virago[1] or sullen, resentful stranger. You are now a fallen idol. From Mum! who could put everything right, you have become Mum! who understands nothing.

Before you throw in the towel, or leap from the bedroom window, or throw your offspring out of the door, find a quiet moment. And consider.

Your child has stepped into a world beyond your reach. The rules, customs, clothes and hairstyles are not within the scope of your experience. Pressures and temptations increase with each decade.

Our teenagers are troubled. They are uncertain. They are emotionally insecure. They are worried about future unemployment, by the continued demolition of their world, by pollution, by the threat of nuclear war. Our teenagers do think, and where rational thought fails to provide solutions, they *feel*. Add to this their burgeoning[2] sexuality, the cynical targeting of youth by the advertising world, and our teenagers are confused and vulnerable.

This is your final and most demanding role as a parent as your children struggle to stand on their own two feet. As a grandmother, here are my tips for survival.

Firstly, I believe that guidelines are still necessary, for your own peace of mind, and to provide your children with a sense of security. But make them flexible.

Talk as one adult to another. Ask for advice sometimes. If you have faith in their opinion – they will too.

Stick to what matters. Teenagers can be rude, fault-finding, arrogant, aggressive and illogical. But try not to become the Opposition. If you turn a blind eye to the vagaries[3] of fashion, then they may listen when what they wear borders on the obscene. Avoid confrontation over the trivial. Avoid confrontation altogether if it's at all possible. Thick make-up, dyed hair and a shaved head are not permanent. A row about drugs will have no impact if last week you raved about purple eye shadow.

It is hard to love a teenager in the full flow of their tantrums but it does not last forever. Be supportive. As their self-confidence grows, you will understand that all the hassle was nothing to do with what you did or said. They are human fledglings trying out their wings. Look on it as necessary, nest-leaving behaviour.

You will both survive, you and your teenager. Ask your own mother.

1: *virago* – aggressive woman
2: *burgeoning* – quickly increasing
3: *vagaries* – unexpected changes

TEXTS

Cut along the dotted lines and staple the texts together to make your own handy anthology. Make sure you keep it safe with your Revision Guide.

TEXT 7

Tom Kevill-Davies is passionate about cycling and food. He has cycled all over the world, eating and writing about food. In this extract, he describes arriving in Ecuador, a country in South America.

***The Hungry Cyclist:* Tom Kevill-Davies**

After another two days of going uphill I arrived in Ipiales and the border with Ecuador. The air was cold and thin. Gasping for breath I said goodbye to a country I had fallen in love with and entered another. From the border, where the usual money changers, pickpockets and disgruntled border officials did everything to make life worse, I rode towards Quito. But in Ecuador it seemed as though someone had dimmed the lights and turned down the volume. Gone were the smiles and friendly cheers of encouragement from the roadside. Gone were the picturesque colonial farmsteads with their flower-covered porches. Here homes were functional, unfinished concrete, spewing construction steel. It rained, it was cold and I wanted to turn around.

Sheltering from torrential rain in a dirty roadside hamlet[1] just north of Quito, I surveyed my options for dinner. A few limp-limbed chickens did another turn in their mechanical rotisserie[2]; a plate of worn-out humitas, a sweet tamale[3], waited for that unlucky customer to save them from another night under the heat lamp; a bored teenager with too much hair-gel prodded and probed a row of disturbingly red hotdog sausages. Not at all tempted by the usual suspects that made up the options in these small Ecuadorian towns, I began to wonder if my hunger could hold out until breakfast.

But hello! What's this?

At the end of the street, sheltering from the rain under a tatty umbrella, an old lady was fanning frantically at the coals of her small grill. I took a seat on the cold steps of the grocery store from which she served, and watched her work while a steady stream of customers pulled in from the rain.

I ordered a bowl of grilled chicken gizzards[4], served on a heap of sweet corn and fried kernels of salted maize and it was immediately clear that she knew what she was doing. As the evening passed by, the buses, trucks and pick-ups splashed through the rain filled potholes of the main street. We didn't talk much, but that seemed normal here in Ecuador, but from what little was said, and my persistent interest in the secret of her giblets[5], it was obvious we enjoyed a common love of food, and it wasn't long before our conversation turned to Cuy. I expressed my dismay at having only found this traditional dish strung up like freshly run over roadkill in front of the tourist restaurants en route from Otavalo to Quito, and my keenness to see how these rodents were prepared at home. I was invited for lunch the next day.

Cuy, conejillo de Indias – Indian rabbits, or guinea pigs as we know them in the pet shop – have been an important food source in Peru[6] and Ecuador since pre-Inca times. Fifteen centuries later, they still remain an Andean delicacy[7], and on average Peruvians and Ecuadorians gobble down twenty two million of these tasty rodents every year. Most Andean households keep cuy at home in the same way that we might keep chickens. Considered a speciality, they are mostly saved for special occasions. Rather like a bottle of champagne or perhaps a box of Ferrero Rocher, a mating pair of guinea pigs are a typical house warming gift for a newlywed couple. Playing an integral role in Andean religious and ceremonial practices, as well as providing dinner, cuy are also used in the traditional medicine of the region. A live cuy is rubbed over the body of someone sick. The cuy's squeaking indicates the diseased area of the human patient.

1: *hamlet* – small village
2: *rotisserie* – rotating spit for roasting meat
3: *humitas, tamale* – local dishes
4: *gizzards* – stomach parts
5: *giblets* – liver, heart, gizzard and neck of a chicken or other bird
6: *Peru* – a country in South America
7: *Andean delicacy* – a favourite food in the Andes, a mountain range in South America

Cut along the dotted lines and staple the texts together to make your own handy anthology. Make sure you keep it safe with your Revision Guide.

TEXT 8

Bill Bryson is an American writer who is best known for his humorous books about travel. In his book Notes from a Small Island *he explores Britain. In this extract, he arrives in the country for the first time.*

***Notes from a Small Island:* Bill Bryson**

My first sight of England was on a foggy March night in 1973 when I arrived on the midnight ferry from Calais. For twenty minutes, the terminal area was aswarm with activity as cars and lorries poured forth, customs people did their duties, and everyone made for the London road. Then abruptly all was silence and I wandered through sleeping, low-lit streets threaded with fog, just like in a Bulldog Drummond movie. It was rather wonderful having an English town all to myself.

The only mildly dismaying thing was that all the hotels and guesthouses appeared to be shut up for the night. I walked as far as the rail station, thinking I'd catch a train to London, but the station, too, was dark and shuttered. I was standing wondering what to do when I noticed a grey light of television filling an upstairs window of a guesthouse across the road. Hooray, I thought, someone awake, and hastened across, planning humble apologies to the kindly owner for the lateness of my arrival and imagining a cheery conversation which included the line, 'Oh, but I couldn't possibly ask you to feed me at this hour. No, honestly – well, if you're *quite* sure it's no trouble, then perhaps just a roast beef sandwich and a large dill pickle with perhaps some potato salad and a bottle of beer.' The front path was pitch dark and in my eagerness and unfamiliarity with British doorways, I tripped on a step, crashing face-first into the door and sending half a dozen empty milk bottles clattering. Almost immediately the upstairs window opened.

'Who's that?' came a sharp voice.

I stepped back, rubbing my nose, and peered up at a silhouette with hair curlers. 'Hello, I'm looking for a room,' I said.

'We're shut.'

'Oh.' But what about my supper?

'Try the Churchill. On the front.'

'On the front of what?' I asked, but the window was already banging closed.

The Churchill was sumptuous and well lit and appeared ready to receive visitors. Through a window I could see people in suits in a bar, looking elegant and suave, like characters from a Noel Coward play. I hesitated in the shadows, feeling like a street urchin. I was socially and sartorially ill-suited for such an establishment and anyway it was clearly beyond my meagre budget. Only the previous day, I had handed over an exceptionally plump wad of colourful francs to a beady-eyed Picardy[1] hotelier in payment for one night in a lumpy bed and a plate of mysterious chasseur[2] containing the bones of assorted small animals, much of which had to be secreted away in a large napkin in order not to appear impolite, and had determined thenceforth to be more cautious with expenditures. So I turned reluctantly from the Churchill's beckoning warmth and trudged off into the darkness.

Further along Marine Parade stood a shelter, open to the elements but roofed, and I decided that this was as good as I was going to get. With my backpack for a pillow, I lay down and drew my jacket tight around me. The bench was slatted and hard and studded with big roundheaded bolts that made reclining in comfort an impossibility – doubtless their intention. I lay for a long time listening to the sea washing over the shingle below, and eventually dropped off to a long, cold night of mumbled dreams in which I found myself being pursued over the Arctic ice floes[3] by a beady-eyed Frenchman with a catapult, a bag of bolts, and an uncanny aim, who thwacked me repeatedly in the buttocks and legs for stealing a linen napkin full of seepy food and leaving it at the back of a dresser drawer of my hotel room. I awoke with a gasp about three, stiff all over and quivering from cold. The fog had gone. The air was now still and clear, and the sky was bright with stars. A beacon from the lighthouse at the far end of the breakwater swept endlessly over the sea. It was all most fetching, but I was far too cold to appreciate it. I dug shiveringly through my backpack and extracted every potentially warming item I could find – a flannel[4] shirt, two sweaters, an extra pair of jeans. I used some woollen socks as mittens and put a pair of flannel boxer shorts on my head as a kind of desperate headwarmer, then sank heavily back onto the bench and waited patiently for death's sweet kiss. Instead, I fell asleep.

1: *Picardy* – an area in northern France
2: *chasseur* – a French recipe, usually made with chicken
3: *ice floes* – sheets of floating ice
4: *flannel* – soft material

TEXTS

Cut along the dotted lines and staple the texts together to make your own handy anthology. Make sure you keep it safe with your Revision Guide.

TEXT 9

This text is from a newspaper article about London's black taxis, or 'cabs'.

***The History of London's Black Cabs:* Ian Beetlestone**

When I picked up my first fare in Covent Garden[1] last month, I couldn't even open the passenger doors. I had two gentlemen fresh from dinner in Langley Street, and I was panicking, pressing all the buttons I could find, fumbling with keys. Nonetheless they were delighted when I told them they were my first, and that consequently the ride – as goes the cabbie tradition – was free, to wherever they wanted to go. Clapham Junction[1], as it happened, though they might as well have said Tuxedo Junction[2] as far as my frayed nerves were concerned.

When I started learning the Knowledge of London in October 2008, the examiner told us it was the hardest thing we would ever do. He wasn't exaggerating. There are no dropout figures, but each year Transport for London (TfL) usually licenses between a quarter and a third of the number of applicants, so we can safely say that most who start the Knowledge never finish it. The average "Knowledge Boy" (or, occasionally, Girl) spends three or four years covering around 20,000 miles within a six-mile radius of Charing Cross[1], out on their moped come rain, freezing wind, or traffic chaos. Hundreds of hours are spent drawing lines on laminated maps of the city, working out the most direct route from hotel to station, restaurant to office, monument to square. We learn thousands of "points of interest", taking in around 25,000 streets. And we don't just sit an exam, we have a potentially endless series of "appearances", in which we recite the perfect route between any two points in the city, until the examiners think we're good enough. I had 19 of them over a period of 18 months – many candidates have more.

The terror of the appearance is legendary – ask any cabbie and watch him wince. In the "olden days", John Mason – head of taxi and private hire at TfL – tells me, the examiners would play games such as putting the chair in the examination room facing the wrong direction, and give an automatic fail to the student who dared turn it around. "You can't do that in the modern age," he says. "I don't think it was acceptable in years gone by, to be frank." Dean Warrington runs the WizAnn Knowledge school that I attended and got his green badge – the licence that allows drivers to operate across Greater London – in 1996. He remembers one examiner who would choose the start and end points of his questions by throwing two darts into a map, and if the student felt this was unfair he would offer to let them throw the darts instead. "He was a crazy bloke." Nowadays the Knowledge seeks to be "as efficient, fair and transparent as possible," says Mason. Well, you can't deny the industry needs to modernise.

And it is doing so. You may not have noticed, but the classic cab is being retired … The Austin FX4 was introduced in 1958, updated and rebranded the Fairway in 1987, and … is set to all but disappear from the streets of the capital in the new year … Meanwhile, hundreds of its successor – the bubblier TX (drivers often refer to it as the "Noddy cab") – have been recalled with mechanical problems and, as you may have read, its manufacturer Manganese Bronze has gone into administration … Fairway driver Lionel May tells me, "You never stop learning", and he turns 80 in January. Will he be sad to hand his Fairway back to the garage? "Most definitely. It goes like a bomb." Everybody I speak to about the Fairway raves about its super-reliable engine that can do well over 500,000 miles without any problems.

Not that that's of much concern to the average passenger who only sits in the back for a few minutes at a time. Aesthetics[3] might be though, and it's a gorgeous car … This was a big part of the attraction for some of us Knowledge Boys – not just the car, but the whole beautiful, archaic[4] industry, first licensed by Oliver Cromwell[5], idiosyncrasies[6] and all. Fellow new driver (we're known as "butter boys" in the trade, because we take the bread and butter from the mouths of established drivers' families) Andrew Baker eulogises[7] this: "I've always recognised the job as being something a little bit special, a little bit unusual, a little bit out of the ordinary." He tells me that when he moved to London to do his degree it was really an excuse to get to the city he'd always wanted to live in, and that it was "romance" that attracted him to the Knowledge, leaving the degree behind. I too was drawn to it in my mid-30s. In love with London and in a career rut, I saw an opportunity to become a working part of this magical town.

…

As my old teacher Dean puts it: "Let's stay the pride of the world's taxi drivers – why not?

1: *Covent Garden, Clapham Junction, Charing Cross* – places in London
2: *Tuxedo Junction* – an area in Birmingham, Alabama, USA
3: *aesthetics* – appearances
4: *archaic* – old-fashioned
5: *Oliver Cromwell* – an English politician and military leader; born 1599, died 1658
6: *idiosyncrasies* – strange characteristics
7: *eulogises* – praises highly

Cut along the dotted lines and staple the texts together to make your own handy anthology. Make sure you keep it safe with your Revision Guide.

TEXT 10 –

This text is from a newspaper article about modern teenagers.

Who'd Be a Paper Boy?

A newspaper round was once a teenager's sole source of pocket money. Not any more, discovers John Crace

It's cold, it's dark and you've got to bolt your breakfast before dragging a bag full of papers round the streets. To add insult to injury, you then have to go to school. So who would be bothered with a paper round? Almost no one these days, it seems.

Twenty years ago, a paper round was one of the few ways for a teenager to earn a few quid to squander on a packet of No 6 and a bottle of cider, and the kids who did it generally took it seriously.

They turned up on time and the right papers were - by and large - delivered to the right houses. Now, a lot of newsagents have given up trying to find kids to do it.

"I stopped deliveries 18 months ago," says Neesa, who just happens to run Costcutter at the top of my road. "I had four boys earning £20 a week for delivering about 18 papers each per day, and every day at least one would fail to turn up and I'd have to deliver the papers myself to stop customers getting angry. It was just more trouble than it was worth."

You can have some sympathy for the kids. Standards in literacy and numeracy have fallen so steeply that it can be a real struggle identifying door names and numbers, and the Sunday papers are now so heavy that your averagely obese teenager just doesn't have the strength or stamina for the job. But the bottom line is that most kids can no longer be bothered to get out of bed for £20.

New research from the Cartoon Network shows that your average kid is raking in £770 a year, of which only £32 comes from paper rounds. Which rather suggests that most teenagers last only about a week and a half in the job before finding it a bit much.

The bulk of the cash comes from pocket money (£186) and part-time work (£256) - selling fags outside the school gates, presumably - but the most telling items are for performance-related pay.

These days, kids extort[1] about £60 a year from their parents for doing household chores and behaving well - both things that used to be just filed under family life.

And if the little darlings can't stretch to a please and thank you, they can always flog a few household items on eBay. Failing that, there's always the tooth fairy.

1: *extort* – get unfairly

Cut along the dotted lines and staple the texts together to make your own handy anthology. Make sure you keep it safe with your Revision Guide.

Images for questions on page 48

Image B

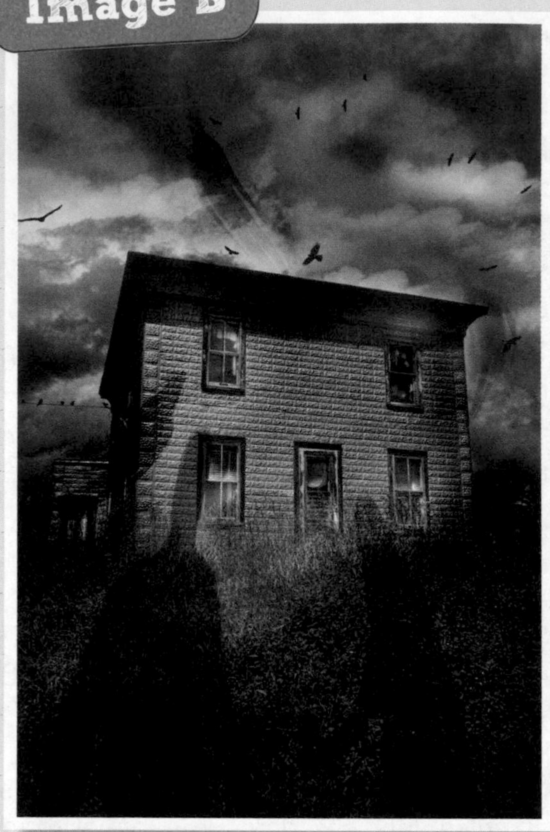

Images for questions on page 61

Image C

Image D

ANSWERS

SECTION A: READING

1 Planning your exam time
Students should spend about 30 minutes on Question 4 (2 minutes per mark).

2 Reading texts explained
For example: The facts and figures suggest that the purpose is to inform readers about teenagers' incomes. These statistics also suggest that the text is aimed at an adult audience, as adults are likely to be more interested in these research findings. The author's point of view seems to be that modern teenagers are lazy.

3 Reading questions explained 1
Explaining how writers use language involves looking at how language and structural features are used and what effects they have.

4 Reading questions explained 2
Paper 2, Question 7 (b) – 'ideas and perspectives about teenagers'
Paper 1, Question 4 – 'attempt to build tension'
Paper 2, Question 6 – 'description of hotels and guest houses'

5 Reading the questions
1 Both (two) texts
2 The whole of each text
3 'Compare', 'ideas and perspectives', 'foreign travel'
4 About 14 minutes

6 Skimming for the main idea or theme
For example: Training to be a cab driver in London is hard work but the job is a magical one and one to be proud of.

7 Annotating the texts
Answers could include:
- 'notched and disfigured bench' – adjectives suggest even the furniture is scarred
- 'rudely hacked' – verb has connotations of violence
- 'old buttons and soup bones' – suggests the prisoners have very few possessions and have to make do
- 'rats and other unseen vermin' – emphasises the unclean environment.

8 Putting it into practice
Answers should identify at least two further points, for example:
- The candle could also be a metaphor as the children watch it melt 'slowly and pitilessly away', which reflects their lack of hope.
- The writer shows Tom attempting to remain positive, but even he loses track of time and gives up shouting, as the 'distant echoes' suggest that help will take a long time to come.

9 Putting it into practice
Answers should identify at least three further points, for example:
- McCourt has washed his clothes in 'carbolic soap' and according to his aunt he smells like 'dead pigeons', which suggests he does not understand how to take care of himself properly.
- He is poorly prepared because he has to be looked after by a 'fat and lazy' aunt who has no experience of looking after boys.
- Despite turning away to hide 'the tears of a man', the fact that he cries suggests he is too young to be starting work.

10 Explicit information and ideas
1 20 years ago
2 £770
3 Cartoon Network

11 Implicit ideas
Answers should include four reasons, for example:
- It takes three or four years.
- The 'appearance' is very difficult to pass first time.
- Not all applicants pass – there are many who never finish the Knowledge.
- Applicants need to spend many hours a week on the training.

12 Inference
Answers should include and explain three short quotations, for example:
- Tom's repetition of 'they will' indicates his optimism but also suggests he is trying to reassure Becky.
- 'A frightened look' and 'a new burst of grief' highlight Becky's anxiety and show she is struggling to cope.
- Tom is 'brought … to his senses', which suggests he is able to think clearly in spite of their situation.

13 Interpreting information and ideas
- 'Office drudge' – as this comes after 'errand boy' and 'porter' and just before the writer states that Lowgood started at the 'very bottom', an 'office drudge' is likely to be a very low-status job, involving taking orders from a lot of people.
- 'Troublesome ladder' – 'ladder' refers to the steps Lowgood has to climb to get to the top, and it is 'troublesome' as he has had to pass through four very low-status jobs before getting a good one.
- 'Pauper orphan' – as this is used as a contrast to 'son of a gentleman', 'pauper' is likely to mean poverty and is used with 'orphan' to emphasise how hard life has been for Lowgood.

14 Using evidence
For example:
1 The writer uses the phrase 'blind eye' to demonstrate the potential mistakes parents make when dealing with teenagers and to suggest it is better to challenge them only on things that really matter. The word 'confrontation' suggests that parents often approach teenage issues in a hostile manner.
2 The writer suggests that parents should avoid confrontations about issues that are not really important as it will be much harder to deal with serious issues that could occur later.

15 Point – Evidence – Explain
For example: Quotation – 'dragging a bag'; Explanation – This suggests that a paper round is hard, physical work, where the load is so heavy that it can only be dragged, not carried.

16 Putting it into practice
Answers should identify at least two further points, for example:
- The narrator is scared he might be trapped by the falling snow, as he says 'it hemmed me in' and describes the snow falling 'thicker, thicker', which increases the tension.
- Verbs like 'lost' and 'quaked' highlight the narrator's fear and sense of helplessness.

17 Putting it into practice

Answers should identify and explain three further points, for example:

- Only 'between a quarter and a third' of applicants are licensed, showing how difficult it is to succeed.
- Applicants need to do around 20,000 miles of practice, emphasising the hard work involved.
- The writer did not have just one exam but 19 'appearances' in front of examiners, highlighting the rigorous nature of the assessment.

18 Word classes

Answers should consist of two sentences and include comments on the use of, for example:

- nouns to emphasise the difference in class between the narrator and Weldon (for example, 'gentleman', 'orphan', 'accountant')
- adjectives before the nouns to emphasise the difference in status (for example, 'pauper orphan', 'bankrupt corn-chandler')
- verbs to show how hard the narrator has worked (for example, 'worked and slaved and drudged').

19 Connotations

Answers should include the literal meaning and the connotation of each word, for example:

- 'hacked' literally means cut roughly; here, it has connotations of repeated, heavy and dangerous thrusts with a knife
- 'taint' literally means having a trace of an undesirable substance; here, it has connotations of poison or danger in the air
- 'slimy' literally means covered in slime; here, it has connotations of unhealthy damp and decay
- 'polluted' literally means contaminated; here, it has connotations of deliberate poisoning
- 'wild beast' literally means an untamed animal; here, it suggests that the imprisoned men are figuratively like dangerous animals.

20 Figurative language

Answers should identify and explain the effect of the two figurative devices, for example:

- 'like a well, like a vault, like a tomb' – these similes suggest that the prison is deep and dangerous, a place that nobody comes out of, a place to die
- 'would have kept its polluted atmosphere' – the personification of the prison suggests that it is cunning and dangerous.

21 Creation of character

Answers should use a P-E-E structure and should identify and explain two examples of how dialogue is used to create character, for example:

- Point – Tom is presented as the leader; Evidence – 'can you bear it if I tell you something?'; Explanation – This suggests he has thought through their situation and has a plan.
- Point – Becky is presented as the more scared of the two as she asks more questions; Evidence – 'would they notice we hadn't come?'; Explanation – The question and answer dialogue shows Becky to be worried and seeking reassurance from Tom.

22 Creating atmosphere

Answers should include three examples of language that creates atmosphere, for example:

- 'unearthly' – adjective suggests a ghost and adds to the sinister atmosphere
- 'spirits of the Fells' – emphasises the supernatural element of the ending of the extract
- 'mocking' – adjective describes the 'spirits', creating a frightening atmosphere that suggests the narrator is actually being haunted.

Answers should also include an overview of the overall mood or tone of the extract. For example:

- The overall tone of the ending of the extract is a menacing one, as the narrator seems threatened by supernatural powers.

23 Narrative voice

Answers should use a P-E-E paragraph structure and comment on the writer's use of third person narrative and its effects, for example:

The third person omniscient narration allows the reader into the minds and feelings of both children. For example, Tom tries to get Becky to talk and he is shown to be reassuring and practical, but the reader knows that Becky is scared even though she says nothing as 'all her hopes were gone'. This omniscient narration shows the reader the difference in reaction between the two children.

(Note that effective P-E-E paragraphs should use adverbials to link and develop the points.)

24 Putting it into practice

Answers should use a P-E-E paragraph structure and could include the following points:

- The connotations of 'pang' and 'agony' are extreme physical pain, which suggests the narrator's extreme fear.
- The build-up of adjectives in the phrase 'long, despairing, wailing cry' emphasises the atmosphere of fear and the hopelessness of the cry.
- References to 'echoes' and 'thickened air' highlight the narrator's isolation.
- The atmosphere becomes sinister with 'unearthly' and 'spirits of the Fells', which have connotations of haunting and suggest real danger.

25 Rhetorical devices 1

Answers should identify and explain other examples of rhetorical devices and could include the following points:

- The alliteration in 'insult to injury' reinforces the sarcastic suggestion that a paper round is hard work.
- The colloquial language of 'kids' and 'fags' helps to build up the idea that the writer looks down on teenagers today as lazy.

26 Rhetorical devices 2

Answers should identify and explain two examples of rhetorical devices, for example:

- The personification of 'worn-out' is used to describe the unappetising food on offer, which elicits the reader's sympathy for the hungry narrator.
- The hyperbole of the phrase 'save them from another night under the heat lamp' adds humour but also a growing sense for the reader of how hard it is for the narrator to find something good to eat.

27 Fact, opinion and expert evidence

Answers should include one fact, one opinion and one piece of expert evidence, for example:

- fact: 'kids extort about £60 a year from their parents'
- opinion: 'Which rather suggests that most teenagers last only about a week and a half in the job before finding it a bit much.'
- expert evidence: 'I had four boys earning £20 a week for delivering about 18 papers each per day, and every day at least one would fail to turn up …'.

28 Identifying sentence types

1 Multi-clause (subordinate)
2 Multi-clause (coordinate)
3 Single-clause
4 Minor

29 Commenting on sentence types

Answers should include one or two sentences explaining the effect of sentence types, for example:
The extract starts with a multi-clause sentence that sets up a tense atmosphere, as the first clause suggests the weather is too bad for the narrator to get home. This is followed by two short, single-clause sentences: the first single-clause sentence simply describes the narrator's sensible actions, but the second changes the mood as it starts with the word 'But'.

30 Structure: non-fiction

Answers should include a sentence explaining the writer's choice of concluding paragraph, for example:

- The text as a whole describes in detail the difficulties of raising teenagers and offers advice on how best to do this. The short closing paragraph offers final reassurance in 'You will both survive'.
- By keeping the final paragraph short, the writer is able to make a key point, reminding the reader that they were once a teenager too in 'Ask your own mother'.

31 Structure: fiction

Answers should include one or two sentences commenting on structure and its effects, for example:

- The use of closely described action reinforces the sense of danger and tension, and allows the reader to experience the events in full.
- The phrase 'distant echoes' foreshadows the disappointment in the following paragraph.
- The repetition of 'and' in the phrases 'and hunger' and 'and ate it' emphasises the slow passage of time.
- The short sentence at the end of the extract reinforces the sense of the children's despair.

32 Putting it into practice

Answers should identify and comment on two structural techniques, for example:

- The paragraph consists of a single, multi-clause sentence, which allows the writer to create a fast pace and build up a sense of the narrator's anger as each clause is added to the last.
- The use of 'and', 'but' and 'so' to link the clauses also links together the steps in Christopher Weldon's successful career, and creates a tone of frustration because the narrator knows that Weldon is successful as a result of family connections rather than talent.

33 Putting it into practice

Answers should include at least two more points, for example:

- The writer starts a paragraph suggesting he has 'some sympathy for the kids', but then follows this short sentence with sarcasm about their lack of stamina, indicating a negative opinion of modern teenagers.
- The repetition of colloquial language such as 'kid' suggests a lack of respect for teenagers.
- The facts and statistics from the Cartoon Network, an expert source, makes the writer's argument believable and trustworthy.
- The emotive language 'extort' makes teenagers sound almost criminal, reinforcing the writer's negative opinion of them.
- The use of the sarcastic 'little darlings' at the end of the extract confirms the writer's viewpoint.

34 Handling two texts

1 Question 7 (b) (the comparison question), which is worth 14 marks
2 Three or four (note: you should also take an overview)
3 Question 7 (b) (the comparison question)

35 Selecting evidence for synthesis

Answers should include one further similarity between the two texts, for example:
Both writers experience unappetising food: Bryson eats 'a plate of mysterious chasseur' and Kevill-Davies observes some 'disturbingly red hotdog sausages'.

36 Synthesising evidence

Answer should include one more paragraph on synthesis between the two texts, for example:
Both writers encounter unappetising food during their foreign travels. In Ecuador, Kevill-Davies is faced with 'a few limp-limbed chickens' and 'disturbingly red hotdog sausages', while Bryson describes 'a plate of mysterious chasseur containing the bones of assorted small animals' he ate in France.

37 Looking closely at language

Answers should identify and explain two further points about language and structure, for example:

- The figures and statistics '20,000 miles' and '25,000 streets' are used to emphasise the difficulty faced by the applicants.
- The pattern of three, 'rain, freezing wind, or traffic chaos', also emphasises the challenge involved in the training.
- Long sentences containing lists of information show how intense the training is by building up a sense of all the requirements.
- The paragraph ends with 'many candidates have more' after a dash, which emphasises how rigorous the assessment is.

38 Planning to compare

Example paragraph:
In the second paragraph of *Who'd Be a Paper Boy?,* colloquial terms like 'a few quid' and 'kids' are used to create an informal and light-hearted tone. They also further emphasise the writer's point that modern teenagers are lazy and spoilt. *Notes from a Grandmother* also takes a light-hearted tone at the start but uses a pattern of three, and hyperbole such as 'leap from the bedroom window', to create this. However, unlike *Who'd Be a Paper Boy?,* which remains sarcastic but light-hearted, the tone of *Notes from a Grandmother* is changed by the use of the short, single-clause sentence 'And consider'. This suggests that the rest of the text will contain advice rather than further descriptions of poor teenage behaviour.

39 Comparing ideas and perspectives

Example paragraph:
Crace's perspective about teenagers remains negative throughout his article and he uses the strong verb 'extort' to put forward his final idea that teenagers are spoilt by their parents. *Notes from a Grandmother*, on the other hand, ends on a positive note, with the idea that, while it is hard to love teenagers, they are just 'trying out their wings'. The writer's use of nesting birds as a metaphor suggests she has a far kinder attitude towards teenagers than the perspective held by Crace.

40 Answering a comparison question

Example paragraph:
Both texts are about teenagers and teenage behaviour, but Crace puts forward the negative view that teenagers are lazy while the writer of *Notes from a Grandmother* is more understanding, describing them as 'troubled'. Both texts use a pattern of three to engage their audience and present their ideas. Crace uses 'It's cold, it's dark and you've got to bolt your breakfast' to establish a colloquial, humorous tone and to set the scene for his sarcastic main argument that modern teenagers are 'little darlings'. Similarly, the pattern of three that begins 'throw in the towel' in *Notes from a Grandmother* is used to create humour, although here it is immediately contrasted with 'find a quiet moment' and the calm advice that follows.

41 Putting it into practice
Paragraphs could include the following points:
- Both writers feel unwelcome: Bryson is treated rudely by a 'sharp voice' at the guest house, while Kevill-Davies finds only unappetising food served by a 'bored teenager'.
- Both writers use adjectives to describe the unappetising food they have eaten on their travels: Bryson has eaten something that looked like 'the bones of assorted small animals' and Kevill-Davies describes 'limp-limbed chickens' and 'worn-out humitas'.
- Bryson's perspective remains humorous. For instance, he describes how out of place he feels, like a 'street urchin', and describes in detail his preparations for spending a night out in the open. On the other hand, Kevill-Davies's perspective maintains a serious tone and concentrates on descriptions of the food, the people and the history of the country.
- Both texts use lists: in *Notes from a Small Island*, Bryson lists the clothing he has to put on to keep warm, which is done to amuse the reader and show how out of place Bryson feels in England. On the other hand, Kevill-Davies uses lists to contrast the landscape of the two countries he has visited. This suggests that he is writing for the serious traveller, rather than to amuse, like Bryson.
- Both writers begin on a negative note but in *The Hungry Cyclist* Kevill-Davies uses a short sentence in the middle, 'But hello? What's this?', to change the tone and to introduce more positive thoughts about Ecuador. In contrast, Bryson remains humorous, but negative, as he waits 'patiently for death's sweet kiss'.

42 Evaluating a text
Annotations could include:
- ideas: 'It was rather wonderful', 'imagining a cheery conversation' – Bryson is obviously anticipating a pleasant welcome, which makes his descriptions of the problems he encounters seem worse
- themes: 'silhouette with hair curlers', 'beady-eyed Picardy hotelier', 'the bones of assorted small animals' – descriptions are exaggerated for comic effect and a humorous tone is created despite the problems he encounters.

43 Evaluating a text: fiction
Answers should identify two points on setting and/or events, for example:

setting:
- danger is suggested by the 'noiseless expanse of black darkness' and the word 'Suddenly' shows how quickly the atmosphere can change
- the descriptions of the snow build in intensity – first it is 'dusky flakes', then it 'hemmed' the narrator in, then it becomes 'noiseless' and 'pitiless'.

events:
- the narrator's actions/thoughts build up and become increasingly desperate – first there is confidence in 'a pretty quick pace', then 'plucked up a brave heart', then the beginnings of worry in 'tried to shout' until, finally, 'terrible, wild shouts', which suggests extreme fear
- the narrator's fear is described in great detail with desperate thoughts of family and home.

44 Evaluating a text: non-fiction
Answers should identify two points, for example:
- The writer describes why teenagers are difficult to live with – they are 'troubled' and 'uncertain', and 'confused and vulnerable' due to their 'burgeoning sexuality' – to encourage parents to be sympathetic towards them.
- Parents are also encouraged to be sympathetic as it is suggested that teenagers are not all bad – they are capable of serious worries about 'pollution' and 'the threat of nuclear war'.
- As she has shown that she understands the reality of living with teenagers, the writer's advice is likely to be interesting and reassuring to parents, particularly as she suggests that 'guidelines are still necessary'.
- The advice is effective as it is presented in a clear and easy-to-understand format – for example, the key point 'Stick to what matters' is followed by details of how to make life with teenagers easier.
- The writer acknowledges that life with teenagers is not easy and that they will still have 'tantrums' whatever parents do; this makes the advice more realistic and interesting to parents.

45 Putting it into practice
Further evaluative points could include:
- events/settings – even when the final candle goes out and 'utter darkness reigned' Tom still attempts to comfort Becky
- the idea of 'heroism' – Tom is presented as a hero as he talks to Becky calmly, does what he can to comfort her and gives confident answers like 'Certainly they will!' to her worries
- the theme of bravery – Tom's bravery is used effectively to contrast with Becky's fear as she cries in his arms; he tries to talk, but 'her sorrows were too oppressive'; her hopes are gone but he tells her that 'no doubt' there is still a search for them.

46 Putting it into practice
Further points could include:
- McCourt presents himself as naïve – for instance, he obviously does not understand that 'carbolic soap' is not suitable for clothes and does not realise that he is being mocked.
- His naivety is also evident when he tells the women it is his birthday rather than saying the day of the week – this is the typical response of a child and shows he is too immature for work.
- McCourt creates sympathy for his younger self when he shows that he is upset by the mocking without understanding the reason for it – he felt his 'face turning hot'.

SECTION B: WRITING

47 Writing questions: an overview

1 Paper 2
2 One writing question
3 Both papers

48 Writing questions: Paper 1

Answers should include at least five or six ideas.

49 Writing questions: Paper 2

- Form: an article (for a newspaper). The writing should include a headline, subheading, short opening paragraph, further detailed paragraphs, conclusion, etc.
- Purpose: to inform the reader about gap years and to explain the benefits of a gap year.
- Audience: probably mainly adults, although younger people and students may also read the article.

50 Writing for a purpose: imaginative

Example paragraph: The rays of warm sunshine raced across the room as I flung back the curtains. Thoughts of the day to come danced through my mind as my eager eyes searched the street for signs of his arrival. I fidgeted impatiently. The syrupy tower of pancakes, the lake of fizzy drink and the mountain of cake were now just hours from my lips.

- Senses: 'warm' (touch), 'searched' (sight), 'syrupy' (taste).
- Verbs to show not tell: 'flung', 'danced', 'fidgeted'.
- Figurative language: 'sunshine raced' (personification); 'tower of pancakes, the lake of fizzy drink and the mountain of cake' (metaphors).

51 Writing for a purpose: inform, explain, review

1 For example: Finding your feet; A typical day; New subjects; What's on the menu?; Extra-curricular activities.
2 For example: I would use an informal tone to appear friendly and supportive, but with Standard English to reflect the form.
3 For example: research suggests the majority of students settle in by the end of the Autumn term; there are typically 20–25 students in a class; lunchtime is from 12.15pm to 1pm.

52 Writing for a purpose: argue and persuade

1 For example: animals are used for personal vanity in the testing of beauty products; many products and medicines could be tested in other ways; animals used for experiments are bred for the purpose and have no quality of life.
2 For example: it is true that human lives are saved by animal testing, but other methods could be used to test the drugs in many cases, for instance, studying human volunteers.
3 For example:
   - Despite campaigns over many years, over 35 per cent of all skincare products are still tested on animals. [Facts and statistics]
   - This involves the cruel torture of a living, breathing being, whose life is apparently as disposable as a cheap tissue from the nearest pound shop. [Emotive language ('cruel torture', 'living, breathing being'), hyperbole ('as disposable as a cheap tissue from the nearest pound shop')]
   - Is 'volume building' mascara really worth the life of an innocent rabbit? [Rhetorical question]

53 Writing for an audience

Example rewritten paragraph: You may think you've got ages to prepare for your GCSEs. You may think you don't need to worry about them just yet. But time flies and it won't be long before you're sitting in that exam hall. So it's important to start getting ready for them now.

[Note the use of some informal features, for example, abbreviations such as 'you've', which are appropriate to this audience but would not be in a more formal text.]

54 Putting it into practice

For example:

- Timing plan: 45 minutes total – 10 minutes planning; 30 minutes writing; 5 minutes checking.
- Form: prose – a narrative (story) in the style of a ghost story.
- Narrative voice: first person.
- Initial ideas: getting ready to meet friends in town; standing next to girl at bus stop; girl leaves coat on seat with wallet inside; miss own bus to take wallet to address; find out girl died three years before; find out bus I didn't take crashed, so 'mysterious stranger' saved my life.

55 Putting it into practice

Answers should include 4-point spider diagrams with ideas, for example:

Question 8 – Form: letter (formal); Purpose: to persuade; Audience: adults; Topic: dirty beaches.

Question 9 – Form: review; Purpose: to inform and persuade; Audience: adults and young adults; Topic: favourite holiday destination.

56 Form: articles and reviews

Answers should include three differences between the formats, for example:

1 reviews use figurative language; articles are more formal
2 reviews tend to give writer's opinions more openly; articles are more likely to use quotations from other people as evidence
3 articles often use quotations from experts to make them seem factual and reliable; reviews are more emotive and personal.

57 Form: letters and reports

1 Letter (formal)
2 Report
3 Letter (informal)

58 Form: information guides

For example:

- Heading – Golden rules for good behaviour
- Sub-headings – Top rules (list); What to wear (paragraphs, possibly a list); Moving around the school (paragraphs); Rules about food (paragraphs); Rules to remember (conclusion, paragraph).

59 Putting it into practice

For example:

- Headline – Teenagers of today: rebels or role models
- Sub-heading – A local teenager reveals the truth about our young people
- Short opening paragraph – It has recently been claimed that the teenagers in our community are agents of trouble, intent on bad behaviour and making a nuisance of themselves. It is a picture many of us are willing to believe, yet does it paint the whole truth?
- Developed paragraph – There are, of course, those who think it does. However, at the end of my road, in a small, unassuming house, lives a young person who defies this image of dangerous delinquent on a daily basis. Jemima Johnson acts not for recognition or for praise, or because she was asked to help. Jemima acts because she has noticed someone in need and has understood that she can make a difference. What does she do? Every day, Jemima accompanies her elderly neighbour to the local shop, providing Mrs Bauer with an arm to lean on, the chance for a little daily exercise and a hand with the groceries. Of Jemima, Mrs Bauer says, "She is an angel. I don't know what I'd do without her". And Jemima is not alone.

60 Prose: an overview

1 Prose
2 Poem and play

61 Ideas and planning: imaginative

Plans should include four or five key ideas and a range of supporting details, including appropriate language techniques.

62 Structure: imaginative

Plans should use the five-part narrative structure and include supporting details about language techniques.

63 Beginnings and endings: imaginative

1 Example paragraphs:
- Opening 1 (vivid description) – The house sat still and silent, squatting low as if to keep out winter's stinging embrace as the dark night pressed forward, its penetrating stare painting the windows black as coal. Inside …
- Opening 2 (dialogue) – "What was that?" squeaked Adam, his eyes wide with fright, his brow furrowed."I don't know," breathed Henry, the quivering syllables leaving his lips in a whisper …
- Opening 3 (mystery) – I know now that it was a mistake. A big one. I should have left things as they were – peaceful, familiar, safe. And yet, that evening …
- Opening 4 (conflict or danger) – A whining creak. A floorboard. Where were they? I could see nothing in the pitch dark and edged around the doorframe into the hall …

2 Ending (to Opening 1) – I was glad, then, and after all that had passed, to be cradled as I was in the peaceful dark. The night was now familiar to me, its hold as comforting as the arms of an old friend. As I stretched out my tired limbs and pulled the blanket closer to me, I closed my eyes, my lips falling into a sleepy smile. It was good to be home.

64 Putting it into practice

Example completed plan:
- Falling action – [describe examining the package and then finding, on the back 'until the morning']; suspect it's from friend, a surprise for tomorrow's trip out; use five senses to describe package.
- Resolution – next morning, open package; it's a silly hat, with a note, from friend to wear to fair as planned; stranger was friend's uncle, who offered to drop off the package; use metaphor to describe hat.

The first two paragraphs of the answer should follow the plan on page 64 and use one or more of the techniques from page 63.

65 Ideas and planning: inform, explain, review

Example plan:
Introduction:
- Give overview of situation – young people have more exams to take than ever before, and schools are under pressure to continue raising grades; this creates extreme stress.

Sub-heading – How teenagers feel and how they act:
- anxious and nervous about the exams
- confused about how to approach revision
- tired due to sleepless nights caused by worrying.

Sub-heading – What parents can do:
- be supportive, not confrontational, if teenagers are rude
- provide healthy food and snacks
- help to write a revision timetable
- give praise when revision is done.

Sub-heading – Support available:
- school year group team
- online revision websites
- older students or siblings.

Conclusion – Finally …:
- plan some kind of celebration for results day
- ensure teenager knows they are loved, whatever the results.

66 Ideas and planning: argue and persuade

Example plan:
- Introduction – hundreds of channels, 24 hours a day, television can dominate.
- Point 1 – TV can be informative/educational.
- Point 2 – shared experience of high-quality drama, etc. (no different to theatre but cheaper and more accessible).
- Counter-argument: some say it takes over our lives; they need to learn how to turn it off.
- Conclusion: like anything, TV is good and bad; it depends on how it's used. Used carefully/selectively it can bring people together, entertain, inform and educate.

67 Openings: transactional

1 Example openings:
- Are you one of those who views skateboarding as a teenage hobby rather than a 'real sport'? Think again.
- Eighty-five per cent of teenagers fail to take the recommended amount of exercise each day; 30 per cent are obese by the age of 15. A skateboard ramp is therefore not an expensive luxury – it is a necessity.
- When I was seven, my parents bought me my first skateboard. It wasn't very expensive, they thought it would just be a weekend wonder. Now I'm the British under-21 champion.

2 Example introduction:

Eight-five per cent of teenagers fail to take the recommended amount of exercise each day; 30 per cent are obese by the age of 15. A skateboard ramp is therefore not an expensive luxury – it is a necessity.

As a nation, we must do something about the appalling state of our teenagers' health. Too many young people are too inactive, they spend hours every day surfing the internet, playing computer games and posting pictures on social media sites. They catch the bus for every short journey, use the lift rather than the stairs and remain motionless all evening in front of a screen. A skateboard ramp could change all that.
[Note that the bold statistical opening has been left as one paragraph to shock the reader. The next paragraph develops the point set out in the introduction, using appropriate techniques: emotive language ('appalling'), repetition ('they') and patterns of three.]

68 Conclusions: transactional

Example conclusion:
A skateboard ramp is neither an expensive luxury nor an unacceptable eyesore, but rather a vital step in encouraging our young people to move away from a static world of immobility and towards a happier, healthier and more active future. Skateboarding may not appeal to everyone, but for some it could make all the difference, helping them to feel fitter and more fulfilled. And isn't a happy, healthy and active life what we want for our young people?
[Note the first sentence of this conclusion summarises the writer's ideas; the second adds a positive note; and the final sentence asks a rhetorical question, further promoting the writer's views.]

69 Putting it into practice

Effective plans will include:
- ideas for an introduction and conclusion
- a range of key points
- some developed detail for each key point
- key points logically sequenced.

70 Paragraphing for effect

As the question asks for a report, paragraphs should follow the third example on page 70 ('Structuring paragraphs: inform, explain, review'):
- start with a clear topic sentence, introducing the reader to the content of the paragraph
- develop the content of the paragraph with further detail.

71 Linking ideas
Example paragraph:
This morning, my sister proved that she is the most annoying person on earth. **For instance**, she finished all the milk so there was none left for me. **Then** she spent an hour in the bathroom. **Later**, she borrowed my headphones without asking and wouldn't give them back. **On the other hand**, she can be thoughtful. **For example**, she made me a delicious lasagne the other day. **Similarly**, she always remembers my birthday and buys me great presents.

72 Putting it into practice
Effective answers will:
- be structured using Point-Evidence-Explain
- sequence and signal their ideas using a range of adverbials.

73 Vocabulary for effect: synonyms
Example rewritten paragraph: The idea of celebrities as perfect role models is not the only misguided ~~idea~~ concept connected with the world of the ~~celebrity~~ famous. Some people have the ~~idea~~ notion that ~~celebrities~~ superstars should be consulted on everything from international politics to haircare.

74 Vocabulary for effect: argue and persuade
Example opening paragraph: In the UK, at this very moment, hundreds of children, some as young as five, are being kept in appalling conditions. They are caged for up to seven hours a day. They are often made to sit in silence while aggressive adults hurl abuse at them. They are subjected to a ruthless regime of punishments. Most shockingly of all, this brutal and barbaric treatment is accepted as normal despite the suffering it causes.
[Note:
- the use of negative emotive language ('appalling', 'ruthless', etc.) to emphasise the paragraph's central idea
- language chosen for its connotations of imprisonment ('caged', 'regime', etc.).]

75 Language for different effects 1
Example extracts for Paper 1, Question 5:
- Rhetorical question – Can you believe such a perfect place exists?
- Contrast – In the harbour, just off the coast of the noisy, bustling centre of Poole lies the peaceful haven that is Brownsea Island.
- List – I walked along the deserted beach, collecting shells, skimming stones and breathing in the salty sea air.
- Repetition – The island was quiet. The island was peaceful. The island was gloriously deserted.

Example extracts for Paper 2, Question 9:
- Rhetorical question – Do you want to live a long and healthy life?
- Contrast – Roaming the great outdoors and breathing lungfuls of fresh air in the sunshine are much more enjoyable than sitting in a stale, airless room staring mindlessly at the television.
- List – Obesity can increase your risk of diabetes, heart attack, depression, arthritis, liver failure, and breathing difficulties.
- Repetition – Exercise can improve your health. Exercise can improve your happiness. Exercise can change your life.

76 Language for different effects 2
Example extracts for Paper 1, Question 5:
- Direct address – You would never believe the pressure my mum inflicted on me.
- Pattern of three – She nagged, pestered and hounded me for days.
- Hyperbole – I thought my head was going to explode.
- Alliteration – This was going to be the most miserable minute of my entire life.

Example extracts for Paper 2, Question 8:
- Direct address – I would ask you to consider the substantial benefits of under-16s being allowed to own a mobile phone.
- Pattern of three – Owning a mobile phone can help under-16s to build a healthy social life, learn to manage the costs involved and stay safe.
- Hyperbole – Preventing under-16s from owning a mobile phone would not only be unfair; it would also snatch from them any chance of a normal life and condemn them to life as social outcasts.
- Alliteration – For parents serious about safety, mobile phones are essential equipment for the under-16s.

77 Language for different effects 3
Example extracts for Paper 1, Question 5:
- Simile – I stared up at her in awe: she was **like a Greek goddess**.
- Metaphor – She **was an oasis of calm** amidst the chaos and clamour.
- Personification – Her **kind words touched** my heart.

Example extracts for Paper 2, Question 9:
- Simile – For many young people, childhood is like a race that should be won as soon as possible.
- Metaphor – Childhood is a rare and precious jewel, which we should treasure.
- Personification – This relentless pressure batters children and their childhood into the ground.

78 Using the senses
Example plan:
- Bed: touch – so many crumbs it feels like the seaside; memory of eating biscuits at midnight.
- Under bed: smell leads nose to under bed; touch – furry shapes turn out to be smelly socks, personify into small animals, huddling together for warmth in burrow made of human hair.
- Chest of drawers: sight – armies of empty deodorant cans, casualties of war; use taste to identify contents of rows of glasses.

79 Narrative voice
Answers could include:
- first person narrator advantages – allows reader to identify with narrator, creates tension as not all events are known by reader
- first person narrator disadvantages – limits the narrative events, gives limited information about other characters' feelings and motives
- third person narrator advantages – allows reader to know everything, can show feelings/thoughts of any character
- third person narrator disadvantages – lacks personal feel created by first person narrative.

80 Putting it into practice
Effective answers should include:
- a counter-argument
- adverbials to link key points and paragraphs
- a wide and varied vocabulary
- simile, metaphor and personification used sparingly
- some use of appropriate techniques, such as alliteration, facts and opinions.

81 Putting it into practice
Effective answers should include:
- a wide and varied vocabulary
- simile, metaphor and personification used sparingly
- some description using the senses.

82 Sentence variety 1
Example sentences:
- Single-clause sentence – My new bedroom is tiny.
- Multi-clause sentence with a subordinate clause – Although I was looking forward to the move, I knew I would miss my friends terribly.
- Multi-clause sentence with a coordinate clause – My brother got to ride in the removal van but I went in the car with the others.
- Multi-clause sentence with a relative clause – Our new house, which is much bigger than the cramped house I grew up in, is in a quiet cul-de-sac.
- Minor sentence – Lovely.

83 Sentence variety 2
Example sentences:
- Pronoun – I was waiting alone in a classroom.
- Article – An eerie silence had fallen.
- Preposition – Beyond the classroom door, I heard footsteps.
- -ing word – Holding my breath, I waited.
- Adjective – Empty and cold, the classroom did nothing to comfort me.
- Adverb – Slowly I realised there was a man standing in the doorway.
- Conjunction – Although I had never seen him before, I knew immediately why he was there.

84 Sentences for different effects
Example paragraphs:
- Life, many people say, is a game for winners and, if you are not a winner, you are a loser who has not worked hard enough or focused clearly enough on your goals. They could not be more wrong. [Note that the first sentence has been intentionally extended using multiple clauses.]
- Whether I'm playing Monopoly, taking a test or running the hundred metres, I always come last. [Note how the key information is placed in the final clause.]

85 Putting it into practice
Effective answers should:
- use a range of single-clause, multi-clause and minor sentences
- use a range of sentence lengths
- start sentences in a variety of ways
- feature sentences structured for effect.

86 Ending a sentence
Example reworked paragraph:
I was born in the countryside **and** I grew up surrounded by the sounds and smells of the natural world. When I was ten we moved to the city. It was a confusing, fast-paced, deafening environment that I found hard to love. It was such a big change – **and** it came as quite a shock to my system. Worst of all I had to leave all my friends behind and try to make new ones in this strange, unfamiliar place. I was lonely **and** convinced I would never feel at home **but** before a year had passed I had the best friend anyone could wish for.

87 Commas
Example sentences:
- A list – A bottle of water, an apple, a cereal bar, a torch and a sticking plaster are all things my mother insists I take with me on every school trip.
- A main and subordinate clause – Although some school trips take us to places that don't interest me, I always learn something new and interesting.
- A main and relative clause – The coach journeys, which invariably make me travel sick and seem to last for hours, are my least favourite part of each trip.

88 Apostrophes and speech punctuation
The corrections are shown in bold.
'There's nothing I can do,**'** said Gary's dad.
'Are you sure?**'** replied Gary.
'I don't know what you mean,' said his dad.
'I think you do.**'**

89 Colons, semi-colons, dashes, brackets and ellipses
1 A colon
2 A semi-colon
3 To add, mid-sentence, information that is extra but not entirely necessary.

90 Putting it into practice
Effective answers should include a range of accurate punctuation including commas, apostrophes, colons and semi-colons.

91 Common spelling errors 1
Are students spotting all their spelling mistakes?

92 Common spelling errors 2
The corrections are shown in bold:
I saw Annabel walk **past** wearing **your** shoes. She was carrying **your** bag **too**. I don't know **whose** coat she had on but it had **two** stripes across the back. She stopped and took it **off**. I don't know **where** she was going or what she was up **to**. It was very strange.

93 Common spelling errors 3
Are students using effective strategies to learn words?

94 Proofreading
Are students spotting errors in their writing?

95 Putting it into practice
Effective answers should contain at least five corrected mistakes.

For your own notes

For your own notes

For your own notes

Published by Pearson Education Limited, 80 Strand, London, WC2R 0RL.

www.pearsonschoolsandfecolleges.co.uk

Copies of official specifications for all Edexcel qualifications may be found on the website: www.edexcel.com

Typeset by Kamae Design, Oxford
Produced by Out of House Publishing

Illustrated by Tech-Set Ltd, Gateshead

First published 2016

19 18 17
10 9 8 7 6 5 4

British Library Cataloguing in Publication Data
A catalogue record for this book is available from the British Library

ISBN 9781447988083

Printed in Slovakia by Neografia

Acknowledgements
The publisher would like to thank the following for their kind permission to reproduce their photographs:

(Key: b-bottom; c-centre; l-left; r-right; t-top)

123RF.com: 106tr; **PhotoDisc**: PhotoLink 106br; **Shutterstock.com**: NikoNomad 106bl, Philippova Anastasia 106tl

All other images © Pearson Education

We are grateful to the following for permission to reproduce copyright material:
Extract on page 100 from *Angela's Ashes*, HarperCollins Publishers Ltd © (Frank McCourt, 2005); Extract on page 101 from 'Surviving the Teenage Years: Notes from a Grandmother' in *A Stranger at My Table: Women Write About Mothering Adolescents*, The Women's Press Ltd (Helen Braid (ed) 1997), reproduced by permission of the editor; Extract on page 102 from *The Hungry Cyclist*, HarperCollins Publishers Ltd © (T Kevill-Davies, 2009); Extract on page 103 from *NOTES FROM A SMALL ISLAND* by Bill Bryson Published by Doubleday. Reprinted by permission of The Random House Group Limited. (Bill Bryson 2015) Penguin Random House LLC; Extract on page 104 from The history of London's black cabs, *The Guardian*, 09/12/2012 (Beetlestone I) The Guardian; Extract on page 105 from Who'd be a paper boy?, *The Guardian*, 11/03/2006 (Crace J) The Guardian; Extract on page 56 from The truth about lying: it's the hands that betray you, not the eyes, *The Independent*, 12/07/2012 (Sherwin, A.); Extract on page 56 from Transformers: Age of Extinction, review: 'spectacular junk', *The Telegraph*, 25/03/15 (Collin R) Telegraph, copyright © Telegraph Media Group Limited.

A note from the publisher
In order to ensure that this resource offers high-quality support for the associated Pearson qualification, it has been through a review process by the awarding body. This process confirms that this resource fully covers the teaching and learning content of the specification or part of a specification at which it is aimed. It also confirms that it demonstrates an appropriate balance between the development of subject skills, knowledge and understanding, in addition to preparation for assessment.

Endorsement does not cover any guidance on assessment activities or processes (e.g. practice questions or advice on how to answer assessment questions) included in the resource nor does it prescribe any particular approach to the teaching or delivery of a related course.

While the publishers have made every attempt to ensure that advice on the qualification and its assessment is accurate, the official specification and associated assessment guidance materials are the only authoritative source of information and should always be referred to for definitive guidance.

Pearson examiners have not contributed to any sections in this resource relevant to examination papers for which they have responsibility.

Examiners will not use endorsed resources as a source of material for any assessment set by Pearson.

Endorsement of a resource does not mean that the resource is required to achieve this Pearson qualification, nor does it mean that it is the only suitable material available to support the qualification, and any resource lists produced by the awarding body shall include this and other appropriate resources.